From Tradesman To Businessman

How Tradesman Make Their First Million In 90 Minute Chunks

David Lee

For Julie, for without her support, I would not have had this exceptional journey. Thanks Hon. xx

TABLE OF CONTENTS

"From Tradesman to Businessman"
"How tradesman make their first million in 90 minute chunks"

Introduction:

So why this book? I have been working within the construction industry for over twenty years now and have seen the industry change considerably over this time. In recent years I have had a great interest in how certain businesses and the people in them make their business successful where others seem to fail. At the time of writing this book we are just starting to come out of one of the hardest and most challenging recessions that the modern day has encountered which started in the early part of 2008 to 2013 with a slow start to recovery at time of writing in 2014. In this time more than 5000 sub-contracting businesses in the UK alone have unfortunately failed. There are many reasons why businesses fail, and I am not here to criticize, as there are many companies out there who have tried their hardest and literally lost everything through no fault of their own.

If you are starting out in your own contracting business or thinking about it then I want you to have the best chance you can. We need to rebuild the construction and contracting sector with quality trades people and to serve our clients with the best service we can. I would like to add at this point, this book is not about how to be the best plumber, electrician, or carpenter, there are

1

other resources for this. This book is purely written to enable you to start and grow your business and turn it into something of a successful and fulfilling business.

About Me;

So I'm guessing you are thinking, who is this guy and what credibility does he have? I know I would be asking the same question, so here's a little about me.

I am a husband and father to two fantastic kids, I have had a normal state education at a local secondary school, with to be honest, what I would call average grades, as I never liked school much. It wasn't until I left school that I really pushed myself. I left at 16 and enrolled for a college course training to be an electrician. Six months into the course I got the opportunity to apply for an apprenticeship, which I was fortunate enough to get. I then worked my way through college for several years qualifying as an electrician and eventually an engineer by the age of 24. I spent eight years working for several large companies developing tools and honing skills at which point I was offered a position as an electrical project manager. Again I moved through companies in this position absorbing as much information as I could on the best practices that each company employed. I was then approached by an old colleague who was starting their own electrical contracting business to assist in building the company up. After five years the company sales figure was over two Million and I decided it was time for a new challenge so I started my own business. At the time of writing the business is in its fourth year of trading with sales of over a million. During the four years I had been approached several times to give advice on similar startup businesses in different trades, some of which I was involved with and have now passed over to others to run. In recent years I have found that I have a passion and drive for helping tradesmen and women succeed in their businesses and hence this book is one part of several products that are available from Tradesman Academy to assist those that want to develop and succeed in their own businesses. I am fortunate enough to have a great team working for me and systems in place where I can spend little time on my existing businesses and concentrate on helping others.

Research:

I have carried out extensive research in the United Kingdom and United States surveying over one thousand people currently working in the trade as a sub-contractor or direct employee to find out what their fears and aspirations are about starting their own business and how best that I could help them. In this book I will cover the main topics that the surveys identified as most challenging to new business start-ups and existing businesses that want to grow.

The research covered the following key questions and I will discuss the two main fears people have as well as covering what I know are the most valuable things you should know from my own businesses that have enabled me to get where I am and enable you to have the lifestyle that you want.

The following is an excerpt taken from the survey:

Fears, Concerns and Attitudes

Respondents were asked to express their biggest concerns regarding running a business and these concerns were grouped together in main themes for the purpose of this report. Overall 44% of all respondents gave a financial answer as a barrier. 29% of respondents were also concerned about competition.

Concern	Respondents %
Financial	44%
Competition	29%
Losing Work	25%
Staff	17%
Other	2%

Respondents were asked to rate a series of potential aspects of business based on how much of a barrier they considered each to be towards running a business. Of all respondents 42% rated financial management to be a strong barrier, this was followed by retaining staff with 41% rating this strong.

Barrier	Respondents %
Financial Management	42%
Retaining Staff	41%
Finding Suitable Staff	38%
Lack of Finances	46%
Lack of Management Expertise	29%
Fear of Failure	28%
Lack of Support	29%
Lack of Experience	24%
Saturated Market	23%
Lack of Marketing Expertise	19%
Red Tape	22%

Barrier	Respondents %
Lack of Finances	46%
Financial Management	42%
Retaining Staff	41%
Finding Suitable Staff	38%
Lack of Management Expertise	29%

Lack of Support	29%
Fear of Failure	28%
Lack of Experience	24%
Saturated Market	23%
Red Tape	22%
Lack of Marketing Expertise	19%

I found this quite an interesting survey as the two most important factors in a new business are financial (Cashflow) which the survey agrees with and secondly marketing.

We will discuss these items throughout this book to educate you as much as I can.

Forward:

This book has been written to provide guidance for those individuals whom are currently in one of two places within their business or career. The first being an individual whom currently works as a tradesman / tradeswoman for somebody else or a company but would like to take the step to start their own business and would like the help and guidance to achieve their end goal. The second being an individual who currently operates his or her own business, however would like to achieve change to the business, whether that be growing the business, more financial gain, or perhaps a better lifestyle balance.

This book covers why you want to start your trade business and the things you need to consider to do so. You have several decisions to make:

- What you are looking at achieving in your business, as there are many factors why people choose to be in business. These are not always obvious and I have personally found that your view on your business changes over time.
- Whether to go it alone or with investors or partners.
- The support you need to run your business, both from your family and professionals.
- The effects it can have on your personal life, both good and bad.
- A plan for the business, where do you see yourself in 2 years' time and what is your long term goal.

To the extent possible, I have written in a manner that corresponds to the Tradesman Academy's users in both the United Kingdom and United States. In the chapters I will use both UK and US annotations. For currency conversions 1 British Pound (GBP) £ is equivalent to approximately $ 1.699 United States Dollars (USD) at the time this Book is authored.

CHAPTER 1
WHERE TO START

If you have it in your mind that you want to start your own business you really need to set a little time aside and think about what you are looking to achieve. Sitting down with your work colleagues or down the pub with your mates, and giving it the "wouldn't it be great to start your own business" and "it would be easy, if he/she can do it, so can I", or perhaps it's, "look at how much money I am making the company, I could do that easily and have it in my own pocket". Well the truth is, you could probably do it, but the reality is, would you do it! I have never met anybody in my working career that has said that running your own business is easy. Never. There are certainly individuals out there that have very successful businesses and you may think they do alright, but the fact of the matter is they took the chance. There are far more people out there that were not that lucky in business and lost everything. I can certainly tell you from personal experience, there are good times in business where you feel you are achieving what you want, but there are also the times when you cannot eat or sleep and you get into a situation where you just want out. Starting in any business is brave and you need to feel comfortable with the crap that comes at you, and it will.

Truth is, there are different types of people out there, ones that like the comfort of knowing they will get their wage or salary at the end of the week or month and know that their mortgage, shopping, and general lifestyle is covered by what they earn. This is comfort for some. Then there are the people who believe in themselves and are willing to take the chance. You need to decide which one you want to be. If you have a mortgage, bills to pay for a family, it certainly isn't an easy decision. I started one of my businesses with less than 2 months' worth of money in the bank as a safety net along with a mortgage, wife and two children, a very scary time but exhilarating at the time as there is more at stake and therefore more determination to do whatever is necessary to succeed.

If you have a partner/spouse then you need to talk to them about your ideas and you need to get them to understand your reasons for starting your own business. Essentially you need to get their full support as there are many times when you come home from work and you need someone to talk to and someone with a clear head on things. Don't forget they will suffer when things are not going right for you as all people need to let their feelings out to somebody which is nearly always your wife or husband. I would always suggest a time frame that you agree on beforehand, so that you give yourself a trial time period say six months and if it's not working out then you sit down and talk through what your next step is.

People tend to want encouragement from others before they start on a venture of a new business, however I can tell you that for some reason and I don't know why, but family and friends have the tendency to try to discourage you from taking the step to go it alone. I really cannot answer why this is, but in my experience and from my involvement with other business owners, it seems to be the norm. Maybe it's because they don't want to see you hurt, disappointed, or some people may just not want to see you succeed. I can honestly say that the only person I look to and has supported me in business 100% has been my wife. She has been a great support in everything that I have done and has always believed in my ability giving me some great advice along the way. Mainly common sense! There are times that you can be so immersed in things that you don't see the obvious and that's where someone else's thinking comes in that isn't directly involved in your business.

Your next step is to write down what you want to achieve over a period of time. This does not have to be set in stone but it serves as a benchmark when you look back overtime to monitor where you are going with your business. Be specific, for example, if you want to grow your business to a certain size, write something like, "In two years I want to employ five electricians, three apprentices and one administrative staff. I want to have my own office set-up with a stores. I want to have three vans on the road. I want to have 30 regular customers etc." You need to keep this list where you can see it regularly as it will have a subliminal effect; nobody else needs to know about it, just you. I can say that I have been able to achieve 90% of what I had written down. Put it in your diary to review the list after a period of time, say every twelve months. Your list will change over time as mine has every time I have reviewed it, but I have always kept my original lists as a benchmark to see how my thinking changes as the business grows. What is your desire?

There's a great book out there called "Think and Grow Rich" by Napoleon Hill, which I would always recommend as a definite read for anybody. The book covers a study carried out over 20 years combing all the essential attributes taken from over 500 hundred of the world's most successful people after which came the following conclusion; there are twelve attributes present in becoming the successful people that they had. Many successful people since have followed these practices. Please note the order of the twelve points and note that the last one is money.

- Positive Mental Attitude
- Sound Physical Health
- Harmony in Human Relations
- Freedom From Fear
- Hope of Future Achievement
- Capacity of Applied Fault
- Willingness to share One's Blessing with others.
- Engaged in a Labour of Love
- Open Mind in All Subjects Towards All People
- Compile Self Discipline

- Wisdom with which to Understand People
- Financial Security

Ask yourself what you want running your own business. Is it your credibility? Spending more time with the family? (This was a big factor for me) Not answering to somebody else? Seeing money earned going into your pocket and not others? Being your own boss? Feeling a sense of worth? Being a valuable asset to your community? Or, deciding what you do with YOUR time!

Without doubt, my biggest reason for starting my own business was twofold; My first reason was I wanted to control my own time, now don't get me wrong, you will do silly hours at times in your business. However, you decide if and when you want to do the hours. My second reason was that I could try my own ideas without having to run them through other people and answering to someone else. Now I only have to answer to myself. If you have bad days in business, which will happen, then you only have yourself to judge and take the blame.
You need to decide what you want your business to do for you?

- You may want to build it and have an exit strategy and sell it on.
- You may want to build a large national business.
- You may want a family business that you can hand down to future generations.

- You may just want to be a one-man/woman business earning enough money to cover your bills.

Whatever it is, you need to decide want you are aiming for, as this is very important psychologically. Whatever it is that you decide, as with everything we talk about, write it down somewhere safe so that you can refer back to it from time to time and benchmark where you are heading. Tip, buy yourself an expensive note book as you are more likely to write in it than waste it!

It is important to set yourself goals with time frames such as you want to go on holiday four times a year, or buy a certain type of car, or buy a certain type of house. Whatever it is be specific, so for example, after five years from starting my business I want a Range Rover Sport in black with cream leather seats and brown steering wheel etc., this will help with your motivation, trust me I am telling you this for a reason.

Your aims will change over a period of time, but you always need a base to start from and looking back at your original aims is a good benchmark for how you are doing in your business and you will also see the mindset changes you will have through your business as it develops. I have changed mine several times and I know it will change several times again which is a normal thing while running your business.

The next step is to decide whether you are going to do this on your own, with a partner, or a joint venture. I would always recommend doing it on your own if you can. Employ people to do the work you cannot and when you need them for the duration of a project. I have been involved with businesses that I have started on my own and with other people. I have met many great people out there to work with, but in my experience if you involve others you will have problems somewhere along the road where one party does not agree on something and the last thing you want in business is disharmony in the camp. It normally comes down to money or one party doesn't feel the other is pulling their weight but are reaping the rewards. Believe me this causes arguments and friction, which isn't good for your business or its customers. You may think that having somebody else involved eases the stress and pressure, but it actually adds to it. Also, if for example there are two of you involved and you make £1,000.00 ($1699.00 US) profit, you will get £500 ($849.50 US) and so will the other person, wouldn't you feel better getting the £1,000.00 ($1699.00 US)? Many people think they do not have the skillset to do all the business activities, however remember you are in a great technical era and you can outsource most things in your business, I do.

Summary of Chapter 1

- Do you want your own business with the highs and lows that come as part of it?
- Do you want a regular comfortable salary at the end of the month or are you comfortable with irregular amounts of money coming in each month?
- Do you have support from your family and the commitment required?
- List your desires and where you want the business to take you?
- List what you want to achieve over a 5 year plan.
- Do you want to go it alone or do want a partner or joint venture?

CHAPTER 2

YOUR BUSINESS STRUCTURE:

We are going to look here at how to start your business and the process you need to go through, I will give you information on both how to do this in the UK and the United States, however there are many similarities, and just as a disclaimer, I am not qualified as an accountant and only offer my knowledge as a point of view from experience. There are different types of businesses that can be started and I will only be covering the types that I believe will suit tradesmen. I would always advise talking to a qualified accountant before you make your final decision.

Choose whether to go it alone or have a partner/partners?

From personal experience, I would always go it alone. It may seem daunting at first and also feels like you have a lot of responsibility on your shoulders, which in a way you do, however there are things to protect you, such as being a limited company as described later on. I have personally gone into two businesses with other people, both have not worked out for various reasons and we have gone our separate ways. I have also questioned many of my business colleagues who have their own businesses and 80% of them would agree to go it alone. If one of the obstacles stopping you going on your own is having someone with a different skill in your company that you don't hold, this isn't a major problem. There is a vast network of resources out there and you can pretty much run your business with what we call virtual assistants, which I will explain a little more about later.

The **top five** problems I see when people consider working with somebody else:

1. If you have two people in the business and you make £1000 profit ($1699.00 USD), you essentially get £500 ($849.50 USD) and so do they. Wouldn't the total amount be better in your pocket?
2. One person always feels they are doing more work than the other person and feel they should get more reward, which can cause friction.
3. All owners of the company have to be in agreement with decisions being made about the company from choosing who you work with to ordering stationery.
4. Responsibility when something goes wrong; It is easy to push responsibility onto somebody else when something goes wrong, which it does from time to time and can cause unwanted disputes.
5. Feeling of responsibility for someone else's finances, we all need an income to pay our bills, and there are times in

business when for one reason or another money may not be coming in. From my experience, this can put you under a lot of pressure when other people's bills depend on your company bringing money in.

I would always say go it alone if you can. I wish somebody had told me this before I started two businesses with business partners. You would have thought I would have learnt from the first one, however I put that down to a one off, but guess what it happened to me a second time! I would really consider my options before I ever went into business with somebody again.

Let's begin with your business structure

Choose a name. Be careful here, your name represents you, your company and its image. You can change it at a later date, however your first name will generally stick with you, and it will cost you to change, not just at company's house or state office, but you will need to change all your stationery, sign written vehicles, clothing etc. This can be an expensive exercise, so try to get it right the first time. Give yourself a time frame and deadline to stick to when choosing your name, say three weeks and that's it or else you will never decide.

Ask friends and family what they think it should be called or put letters of your family's names together, I have generally named my businesses from using letters out of my children's names, doesn't really matter, however in needs to be legal, available (which can be checked easily on the internet) and most of all sensible. I know a few people that have called their company names they thought were funny or entertaining and what tends to happen in this case is that people may not tend to take you seriously.

Another tip is to try and get a locality name such as Birmingham Plumbing. The only problem is that you may find it difficult to obtain these types of name as they go quickly. However you can normally find some sort of variant. This type of name is great for your business as it helps massively with your marketing, which will be explained in a later chapter.

Choose what type of company to start. As mentioned previously there are many different types of companies. I have separately outlined below the structures in both the United States and the UK. In the United States the country is broken up into 50 states and each state has different laws, so this will need to be checked with your accountant, the states have similar requirements, however these vary slightly in the respect of cost in filing the information, for example in Pennsylvania it may cost $125 USA or £ 73.57 (GBP) whereas in California it may cost $100 or £ 58.85 (GBP) The requirements for each state are on each states home page, typically on the Department of State or Secretary of State's page for a specific area. In the UK you can use Companies House or there are several companies that will do this for you for a cost on the internet, typically costing you from £25 ($42.47 USD) upwards depending what you require from them.

Business Structures in the United States

It will be the responsibility of the business owner to select the entity type as the choice will affect the businesses tax liability. However, the following should give you a basic understanding of the selections one has available to them.

The basic structures are:
- Sole Proprietor
- Limited Liability Company (LLC)
- Corporation
- S-Corporation
- Non-Profits

Sole Proprietor is the most basic and is essentially an individual that pays a nominal fee to the state in which they reside to operate as a business under his or her own name or a business name.

Here is an example: Bill files to operate as a sole proprietor under the name Bill's Lawn Care. All revenues generated from that business go directly to Bill and he simply claims whatever he earned on his tax return and pays the appropriate amount. Fairly straight-forward.

The problem is Bill is not protected from a liability stand point, so should something unfortunate happen Bill would be personally liable.

Partnerships - A partnership is the relationship existing between two or more persons who join to carry on a trade or business. Each person contributes money, property, labor or skill, and expects to share in the profits and losses of the business.

A good example here would be a real estate development company where you have one individual who is knowledgeable in construction and another who has expertise in sales or leasing. These two individuals might partner up where one is responsible for the construction aspect and the other for the sale or leasing of the finished project.

Limited Liability Company (LLC) - Owners of an LLC are called members and/or managers depending on how one file's with the state in question. Most states do not restrict ownership, and so members may include individuals, corporations, other

LLCs and foreign entities. There is no maximum number of members. Most states also permit "single-member" LLCs, those having only one owner.

Depending on elections made by the LLC and the number of members, the IRS will treat an LLC as either a corporation, partnership, or as part of the LLC's owner's tax return. Specifically, a domestic LLC with at least two members is classified as a partnership for federal income tax purposes unless it files IRS Form 8832 (Entity Classification Election) and affirmatively elects to be treated as a corporation.

*The popularity with an LLC is that there are no Federal Income Taxes paid by the company, instead the tax is passed through to the members. So if ABC LLC has earnings of $1 million dollars (£ 588,594 GBP) that money will be claimed as income on each member's tax return.

Corporation - In forming a corporation, prospective shareholders exchange money, property, or both, for the corporation's capital stock. A corporation generally takes the same deductions as a sole proprietorship to figure its taxable income. A corporation can also take special deductions.

For federal income tax purposes, a corporation is recognized as a separate taxpaying entity. A corporation conducts business, realizes net income or loss, pays taxes and distributes profits to shareholders.

The profit of a corporation is taxed to the corporation when earned, and then is taxed to the shareholders when distributed as dividends. This creates a **double tax**. The corporation does not get a tax deduction when it distributes dividends to shareholders. Shareholders cannot deduct any loss of the corporation.

Starting the Business

So, in this example I will use Pennsylvania, but you can interchange any location you see fit. The two most popular choices are Limited Liability Company and Corporation. The example will be for a corporation, but an LLC is basically the same.

Today most if not all states allow for online filing, and it is much more convenient, so I suggest that route.

Step 1) Go to the appropriate web site for the state in question (This was addressed at the start of this document).

Step 2) Do a name availability check. If the name is available proceed. If it is not available you will need to select a different name. The name check is available on the same website.

Step 3) Once you have the name you complete the related forms for the creation of a corporation in that state. There will also be directions available that will instruct you if there is the need for additional actions that are needed aside from the form you are completing at the moment. An example of this is the publication requirement mentioned earlier.

Step 4) Submit the application with the appropriate filing fee.

*Note: The business is created when the payment is processed, not when the paperwork is received in the mail. One can file on March 1st and receive the paperwork on April 1st, but the document will state that the entity began on March 1st.

EIN - The registration process is finished where the state is concerned. The next step is to apply for an Employer Identification Number (EIN). This is a unique number issued by the IRS that identifies a business.

It can be filed online or one can submit an IRS SS-4 form (Application for Employer Identification Number). If done online a number is generated immediately upon submission of the form.

Tax ID - A Tax ID number is simply one's social security number. A sole proprietor would use their social security number.

The Corporation Package – Both corporations and LLC's use the same packages with minor differences, for example a corporations package will include stock certificates whereas an LLC will contain membership certificates.

These packages contain those items that are required to make a business technically legal such as:

- Stock or Membership Certificates
- Corporate Seal

- Minutes Book

These can be purchased on line or at most stationery stores that sell legal supplies. Most states require minutes to be kept but there are no requirements to file any minutes with the state. These packages are rather inexpensive.

Company Bank Account – The final step is the company bank account, which needs to be opened by an officer of the company. The officer who must be able to present the original papers issued by the state showing that this is in fact an actual business, and even more importantly that this individual is authorized to open the account.

The individual will also be required to have a social security number. For a non-U.S. person, one or more of the following: a taxpayer identification number, passport number and country of issuance, immigrant identification card number, or number and country of issuance of any other government-issued document evidencing nationality or residence and bearing a photograph or similar safeguard.

Becoming a Contractor

Per your request let's say that the business started above was for a General Contractor located in Philadelphia, Pennsylvania. Let's also assume that the company will be operating legally with all of the required licenses and permits.

After the company is created the next step would be to apply for all of the required licenses to operate a business in the city or town in which it is registered or is looking to provide services.

The first step is to complete and submit the application. The application is provided by the Department of Licenses and Inspections and is required for any company doing business exceeding $500 (£ 294.29 (GBP)).

Every location will have its own rules and regulations, but the local building authority will issue most if not all licenses.

The various other business licenses would depend on the type of contractor and the services offered, but local governments provide businesses with information on what licenses they will need to have for their specific business.

Tax

The United States has a sales tax and that tax is implemented by the state. Additionally, many local governments add their own amount on top of that. Pennsylvania for example has a 6% tax on most items, but if you buy something in Philadelphia you can expect to pay the 6% state plus an additional 2% local tax.

Anyway, if a contractor also sells items (in addition to providing services) he will have to secure a license that allows him to collect sales tax.

So, say you have an electrical contractor that also has an area of their shop where they sell generators. They will need to collect a tax on the sale of each generator that tax is then paid to the state, and in some instances to local governments on a monthly, quarterly, or annual basis.

Business Structure in the UK

In the UK there are several companies that you can set up. Most businesses in the UK are:

- Sole Trader
- Limited
- Limited Liability Partnerships
- Partnerships

Go to: www.gov.uk/business-legal-structures/overview for further information.

The two main company structures I would suggest you consider are:

- Sole Trader &
- Limited

I have given a brief outline of what I think you should be aware of in both cases and further information should be sought from a legal advisor should you need further advice as each has difference tax implications and regulations.

Sole Trader Structure - An example of a sole trader would be a taxi driver who has little risk in his business if somebody doesn't pay him. As a sole trader (You) have responsibility to pay all its debts even if you don't get paid. So if the taxi driver has somebody not pay a fare they will be left with a small out of pocket expense and say if this happens ten times per year and has cost an average of £20 ($33.97 USD) per time then essentially the taxi driver has lost £200 ($339.79 USD) of income which wouldn't affect his business.

If a plumber is in business as a sole trader and has 6 clients that don't pay him over twelve months at an average cost of £3,000 ($5096.89 USD) then the plumber will be in debt of £18,000 ($30,581.35 USD) The plumber will still have to pay for labour on the job, i.e. your wages and also any materials which could have a big impact on your business and could end up with the business folding with the debts still owed.

Limited Company - A limited company can be thought of as a person in their own right, so if the company had payment problems, then the debt wouldn't be passed to the individual as long as the correct business practices have been carried out. i.e. the company limits your responsibility to how its run and the money owed. You must operate within the rules of a company business though as you may be liable for the company if you don't.

For both the sole trader and limited companies there are different tax allowances and people tend to choose which company they go with by how much they will be able to earn from the company and the tax they pay efficiently. Therefore you may be better off tax-wise being a sole trader but you also need to be aware of the implications should you have outstanding debts, again I would advise you to talk to an accountant about this.

On a personal note, I have always set companies up as limited as this suits how I want to run my businesses.

Tax – Corporation tax and value added tax (VAT)

Corporation Tax - A business in the UK is required to pay its share of tax, this differs between sole trading companies and limited companies. In short, if you are a sole trader you will be paying tax on your earnings, and if you are a limited company you will be paying corporation tax on profits the company makes after it has paid all outgoings including wages of employees. There are pluses and minuses to both limited and sole trader companies and I would advise you to seek advice from an accountant. I will give the following example of how a limited company would work tax wise as this is what I have always set my companies up as; let's say I have a painting and decorating company that has sales of £160,000.00 ($271, 834.23 USD) over a financial year. I have spent £45,000 ($76,453.37 USD) on supplies and labour and I have overheads over the year of £60,000 ($101,937.83 USD) giving a total outlay of £105,000.00. ($178,391.21 USD) (Note I haven't taken a wage yet). This leaves me £55,000.00 ($93,443.01 USD) for which the company is taxed on at 20%, therefore you would be left with £44,000.00 ($74,754.41 USD) in the company which you can do what you want with. You would then be allowed to take a dividend of approximately. £34,000.00 ($57,764.77 USD) (Variable at time of writing) without paying tax personally. (Note, there has to be enough money in the company to do this or they become illegal dividends, which would cause you a problem.) You would also be sensible to take a minimum wage weekly or monthly of approx. £8,000.00 ($13,591.71 USD) per year to cover your minimum NI government allowances, which again is essentially tax free.

VAT - Most businesses in the UK will be required to pay VAT when their business reaches the VAT threshold, which is currently at £79,000.00. Therefore, if your company turns over more than this in a year you should be paying VAT.
I wouldn't advise trying to ignore it, Her Majesty's Revenue and Customs (HMRC) will catch up with you.

There are problems with being VAT registered as you can put yourself in an uncompetitive position depending on your market. For example, if you're looking to grow your business to a larger concern to say turning over £1 Million per annum ($1,698,963.97 USD) then you will be VAT registered and therefore will pass this VAT cost onto your customer. Where the problem lies, is if you are targeting say house rewires at £3,500 ($5,946.37 USD) per house and you are VAT registered the cost will actually be £4,200 ($7,135.64 USD) Now if you are competing against somebody who isn't VAT registered, which you will be, and essentially the customer gets the same job whichever company they go with, then most people with go for the cheaper quote. This is a problem and unfortunately there isn't much you can do about it as the tax system stands at the moment. My businesses are all VAT registered, and yes I do loose some work, however when you get a good reputation for your workmanship, you will find that a lot of customers will be sold by your service and not cost. Your reputation takes a time to build and I would always suggest not to get VAT registered until you reach the VAT threshold, and only then have a long hard think about it and speak to your account as it will affect your conversion in sales.

What else you should know about VAT? There are different types of VAT in the UK, the two types that you would consider as a contractor would be:

- Standard Rate VAT
- Cash Accounting VAT

Okay, so why does it matter which one I go for if I decide to become VAT registered. Well, the main difference between the two types is that standard VAT relates to invoices in and out at the date of the invoice, and cash accounting relates to when the goods are actually paid for. So for example, if you do your VAT as standard rate and the invoice you send to the customer is dated to be paid on the 25th of the month, the revenue department will have expected you to have obtained this money by then and you will be liable to pay the amount of VAT on the invoice against your VAT bill. This is fine as long as you have been paid on time. In the real world, there are very few companies that pay on time and you may not get paid for a further 30 days following the invoice due date or may not get paid at all if there is a dispute. What cash accounting enables you to do is pay VAT when you have made payment to a supplier or received payment from a client which will assist in your cash flow greatly. It is my personal preference to go with cash accounting as opposed to standard rate as it will help with cash flow in your business.

Where you work from:

So where are you going to base your office? Start small, you can always expand. You have options where you work from each having plus and minus points. The first office I worked from I rented and was approximately 3.65m X 2.74m (12ft x 9ft) and very warm in summer!

Consider the following options:

- Work from home
- Rent an office
- Rent a virtual office space (Hot Desk)

Option 1

Work from home – I would say this would be your best option when starting your business as it will keep costs down initially. If you find you need extra space after six months, then you will have a better understanding of where you are going financially in your business at that point and if the work you are undertaking warrants the overhead of an office. I will list some of the overheads you need to consider when renting an office below:

Plus points - cheaper than renting or buying office space and will give you time to work on other areas of your business until you are properly up and running.

Minus points - Distraction, whilst at home it is very easy to get distracted. When you are away from home in an office environment, you very much have the mindset to get your work done and not take the dog for a walk, read the paper, or relax in the garden.

Be mindful if you do work from home to consider using a PO Box address. This enables all your correspondence to go to your local post office, which you then either get picked up or you can get delivered. Otherwise you will end up having a lot of unwanted mail and perhaps sales people knocking on your door at your home address. There is a downside to PO Boxes. A PO Box can sometimes give the client an impression that you have something to hide and for some reason you do not want to be able to be contacted directly.

Renting an Office: You need to consider the size, obviously the bigger it is, the more rent you will pay, so you don't want to be paying out a lot initially for space you are not using. Do you need a store? I would advise looking for something initially when you have enough room for the people you know you are going to need in the business, say yourself and an administrative assistance and then allow yourself additional area of space to take on a further person if needed at a later date. Try to give yourself an area where you separate your daily work (possibly at your desk) from an area that you use for quoting and tendering jobs. Drawings and paperwork can get cumbersome and take over your desk, so try to keep areas separate.

Location of your office is crucial. Think about your travelling to and from the office for you and your operatives. Do you want them stuck in traffic all the time costing you money? Try to get close to main A roads and motorway networks when possible.

Will your clients be coming to your building? If your clients are going to see your building, you need to consider how they perceive it. Remember your image will go a long way to whether your potential clients give you the work or not.

Costs you need to be mindful of when renting:

- Initial deposit – can be up to six months
- Monthly cost of renting from landlord
- Business Rates
- Telephone Bills
- Internet Charges
- Electricity Bills
- Gas Bills
- Buildings Insurance
- Office Equipment – Computers / Desks etc
- Cleaning
- Service Charges by Landlord

Plus Points - Your clients will see that you have a structure to your business. Work and home life can be kept separate. When you are working from home, this can become difficult as it is easy to pop into your spare room/office and carry on with work when you should be spending time with your family. It is easier to employ staff working from your office rather than from your home.

Minus points – The cost of running your office.

Virtual Office: What is a virtual office? There are many companies that offer a service as a virtual office. This is where you can utilize somebody else's building from just renting a sole desk in an office to renting a room in the building along with telephone line and internet. The advantage of this, is that you have a range of facilities that you can use in the building if you need them. So for example, you can use their reception to answer your calls and take messages, thus giving the impression that you are more established than you actually are. They also offer meeting rooms which can be great when a potential client comes to visit you. You do not need to take them to your desk or office area, you can meet them in a designated meeting room with facilities provided for you. Of course these facilities come at a cost but you can find some very good deals out there, which will result in only paying for facilities when you need them. This helps with your cash flow until you are in a position where you want to move to your next premises.

Advantages of a virtual office:
- Receptionist provided to take calls if required
- Meeting rooms provided as and when you need them
- No building maintenance expense
- One cost per month to cover everything you need
- Good impression to your potential clients

- You are able to hire more desks or office space as you grow without moving location.

Disadvantages of a virtual office: 1) More costly than working from home, 2) more difficult to find places that also have storage areas for materials and plant that you may hold as a contractor.

Summary of Chapter 2

Choosing your business structure is an important decision for you, your business, and it's operations. You will need to decide whether you want to own your business by yourself, with a partner, or with a group. I suggest and recommend structuring as an individual.

The business structures in the United Kingdom are Sole Trader, Limited, Limited Liability Partnerships, and Partnerships. Each of these has its own applications and benefits. I recommend Sole Trader or Limited structures.

The basic structures in the United States are Sole Proprietor, Limited Liability Company (LLC), Corporation, S-Corporation and Non-Profits. As an individual, the
Limited Liability Company (LLC) affords you the best liability protection as a single owner. All of these structures have different rules for purposes of taxation.

CHAPTER 3

WHO YOU HANG ABOUT WITH MATTERS.

Networking and strategic alignment - Studies have shown that who you hang around with makes a difference to your work and personal progression. Now, don't for a minute think that you have to sack all your friends and associates. You just need to understand, focus, and invest your time with those people that will enhance your business or your life. You would be surprised how many people have a negative effect on you without you even knowing it. It may be for several reasons, let's look at what I would say are the four categories of people I am referring to:

Your family - Okay, you are not going to sack your family, well I hope not anyway, but I would tread carefully how much you get your family involved in your business unless obviously they are part of the business. As in a previous chapter, my wife is a big help with me in my business. She is the only person in my family that I discuss my business with, for two reasons. 1) There will be times when you have a lot going on in your mind and you may seem distant or focused when you are spending time with your family and they need to know that you are like you are at that time because of your business and not because of your personal life.

Many people say when you leave work at the end of the day you should switch off and focus on what's happening in your personal life. This is a great thought, but in reality, I know very few business owners that do this as you are constantly thinking about things that are happening in your business. 2) She isn't involved at all in the business and therefore has the ability to take the helicopter view (looking from above at the grand scheme of things) about what I discuss with her which can be a great help. However there will be times in your business when you need to take risks, calculated ones most of the time, but there are times where you tend to go with your instinct. Now if you put an idea you have out to your family for an opinion, you will find a lot of the time that you will get a negative reaction, mainly because they think you are taking a risk they wouldn't feel comfortable with, and not necessarily that you would feel uncomfortable with.

Your Friends - I'm sure like me you have many friends and acquaintances that you have met over the years possibly going back to your school years. I would discourage you to hang around with the one's that let's say have habits that may not be congruent with yours such as drinking 7 nights of the week or cheating on their partners as things like this can make you feel that this is the norm and you are also okay doing these types of things. You have to ask, is this how you want to position yourself? Remember when you were in your teen years and your parents would say don't hang around with him or her, as they will lead you down the wrong path and get you a reputation as other people will associate you with this person and also associate their habits with you. Choose your friends wisely, I can honestly say that I have quite a few friends and associates, but there are less than a handful that I would truly call my friends and would invest my time with on a regular basis.

Work and Business Colleagues - This is the one that I find most interesting, I have amassed a wealth of information and knowledge in my industry over the past 20+ years to get me to the position I am at today. I am very grateful for the knowledge and experience I have gained without which I'm sure I wouldn't be the person that I am. However, the majority of people you work with or other business owners really don't like to see you develop your business. It is rare to get any positive comments from them, they all tend to be negative and I really don't know why, it just happens, the only thing I can assume is that they do not want to see you succeed and possibly do better in business than they do. I have had a few experiences of others trying to take a knock at both myself and the companies I am involved with.

If there is one crucial thing you take away from this book it is the following:

"Be careful who you trust, as there are people out there that want you to fail."

So what do you do about these negative people? You distance yourself from them, take a distance view on how they operate and pick out the good and bad and use this knowledge to develop your skills. Surround yourself with people that are like-minded to you and are on the same path. Involve yourself within a forum of like-minded people on the internet or join a local group of business owners in your area. I did this and it became one of my most valuable sources of information.

You should always look to educate yourself, never stop learning, we live in a world where it is so easy to obtain information and grow your knowledge and experience. I'm a great fan of books of which I normally read one per month. If your thing is not reading, then get audio books to listen to in the car or on your IPhone, IPod, etc., There is no excuse these days, always continue to educate yourself it will be what stands you out from the majority.

Summary of Chapter 3

Studies have shown that who you hang around with makes a difference to your work and personal progression. Do you want to work with family, friends, work colleagues, or business colleagues? Be careful who you chose as some want to see you fail. Distance yourself from the negative. What you have to ask yourself when pondering a business is "Who will truly support me?" Who has a vested interest in your success? The four categories of people I refer to support your success in this order; family, friends, work colleagues, and business colleagues. Immediate family will

41

support you the most. You may have some very close friends but also remember finances and stress affect everyone differently. I am confident you have heard stories about breakups of business partnerships and friendships over differences in opinions on how the business should be run or situations of financial struggles. One partner may have the business skills the other the trade skills but both disagree on daily operations of the business. I am very grateful for the knowledge and experience I have gained from work and business colleagues, however, the majority of people you work with and other business owners really don't like to see you develop your business.

If there is one crucial thing you take away from this book it is: "Be careful who you trust, as there are people out there that want you to fail"

CHAPTER 4

USING TRIED AND TESTED METHODS

Learn from other's mistakes. The concept behind Tradesman Academy is to provide you with the right information before you start to minimise the mistakes that you will encounter on your journey. A bit like having a road map, or Tom-Tom before you start a journey in your car, as it will guide you to your destination via the best route and steer you clear of problems you may encounter on the way. To begin, let's look at an example that we all know about. It calls itself: "The Most Successful Small Business In The World" This one is actually a franchise but it's the way it started and grew that is important.

Have you heard of a guy named Ray Kroc? This guy was a 52-year-old sales man who was in the process of selling two brothers a milkshake machine for their hamburger stand in San Bernardino, California. You now know what Ray Kroc developed from this encounter as McDonalds. Although simple as you may think now, he realized that these two brothers produced hamburgers quickly, cheaply and in an identical fashion. This essentially was a money machine as anybody could do it with the correct training. We all know how large McDonald's is now and how well it stands in the market place. Everybody knows the name.

Now I am not suggesting you go out and buy a Franchise, that's totally up to you. However, you need to understand that you have to invest heavily into a Franchise, typically well over £100,000 ($169,896.39 USD) and there is the fact that you need to give a set amount of profit back to the Franchise owner on a regular basis to allow you to use their brand and their systems, which are proven to work.

So what's the importance of you understanding that a Franchise model works? According to an excerpt from the top selling business book "The E Myth" by the small business Guru Michael E. Gerber the following is to be noted
"According to studies conducted by the U.S. Commerce Department from 1971 – 1987, less than 5 percent of Franchises have been terminated on an annual basis, or 25 percent in 5 years. Compare that statistic to the more than 80-percent failure rate of independently owned businesses and you can immediately understand the power of the turn-key revolution in our economy."

This statement identifies that having a proven format and business structure for you to follow gives you a greater chance of making your business succeed. One thing I must point out at this stage is that Tradesman Academy is not a Franchise nor is it looking to sell its brand. What it is though is a business platform that will guide you through the steps of your business similarly to that of a Franchise giving you the benefits that a Franchise has to offer without the cost. Essentially, you can call your business whatever you want and use the information provided by Tradesman Academy in your business. This way the business is entirely yours and all your profits go in your pocket and not somebody else's. If you want the services of Tradesman Academy you simply purchase what suits your business model to drive your business forward.

These are some of the tried and tested methods to get your business off the ground. Additional assistance may be sought in chapter 14.

Wholesaler interactions – Open an account with at least three wholesalers for your particular materials, as you need to be getting competitive pricing when you are pricing to your customers. I would also try and get wholesalers that are close to your offices as there are times you will need to pick things up and you don't want to have to travel long distances to pick materials up for a job. Yes most companies deliver, but there will be times where you will need to go and pick something up.
As you are a new company, it will be hard for you to get credit. Most wholesalers will allow you a credit limit initially of around £3,000 ($5,096.89 USD) until you have a proven track record or your first year accounts behind you. Tip, always do your best to pay your accounts before they are due or on the due date, try not

to let them go overdue. This sometimes happens, but you will build a better relationship with the wholesaler if you generally pay on time and they will be more forgiving when you need to pay past your due date as long as you are honest with them.

Personal guarantees - Your wholesaler may ask you for a personal guarantee to give you an amount of credit. This is normal for a new business, however you need to be aware that a personal guarantee is what is says even if you are a limited company. If the company doesn't pay its bills, then they can come after you personally. Where you have to be careful with personal guarantees is when the wholesaler raises your credit which also reflects in your personal guarantee, so for example, you have taken a credit amount out with Hill plumbing wholesalers, for £3,000 ($5,096.89 USD) and you have had to sign a personal guarantee. The wholesaler then says to you after 6 months of you paying your bills on time, that they will raise your credit to £15,000.00 ($25,484.45 USD) which helps you and your growing business. However your personal guarantee also raises to this amount unless you get it in writing from them that it doesn't so be careful. I have been caught out by this myself.

Credit terms - When you set up your account you will generally get 30 day credit terms, meaning that you are required to pay the bills 30 days following the receipt of goods. It is worth knowing that a lot of wholesalers will give you 60 days terms, which will help your cash flow, but again you need to demonstrate a proven track record before they will consider this.

Summary of Chapter 4

Tradesman Academy was developed to provide you with the right information before you start your trade business to minimise the mistakes that you will encounter on your journey. You need to decide the business platform you want to own. Use the tried and tested methods of previous business owners such as Ray Kroc. Start small and build a reliable model, which is consistent. There are three methods to get your business started; Wholesaler interactions, Personal guarantees, and Credit terms. Using wholesaler methods to start your business you will open an account with at least three wholesalers for your particular materials as you need. Most wholesalers will allow you a credit limit initially of around £3,000 ($5,096.89 USD) until you have a proven track record or your first year accounts behind you. If you are using a personal guarantee line of credit a wholesaler may require a signature for the loan. This type of loan is based on your trustworthiness or credit rating and does not require collateral. Be aware this method is what is says even if you are a limited company. You are responsible. Credit terms help you to establish your business by establishing accounts. When you set up your account you will generally get 30 day credit terms, meaning that you are required to pay the bills 30 days following the receipt of goods. It is worth knowing that a lot of wholesalers will give you

60 days terms, which will help your cash flow, but again you need to demonstrate responsible management of the funds.

If you need additional ideas for funding and financing, a business plan is provided in chapter 14 Business plan development for new construction company owners. It will walk you through the required documentation to acquire loans from lenders including marketing plans, historical information, future plans and the required financial information for current and future projected income as well as references and other supporting documents.

CHAPTER 5

HOW TO MAKE THE JUMP FROM YOUR CURRENT JOB

So how do you get started and make the jump into your new business? This really depends on where you are currently positioned. If you are already out of work then this is pretty straight forward as you have no other work commitments. I am going to tell you how I started my first business as I was employed by a company.

The first thing is don't go after clients that the company you are employed by has as it is unethical and can also get you into problems legally. Also, some of the clients your old company have will not be very impressed as you will come across as an untrustworthy person. There is nothing wrong with approaching these clients after a period of time following you leaving your old company, just leave it a minimum of six months before you contact them. By the way, there is nothing wrong in advising your clients you are leaving when you have announced it at work. If they want to keep in contact with you, they will ask you for your details. A bit of advice, if you are planning to leave in six months from your employer, don't drop your standards at work. Work to your best ability, as if you impress their clients so much, those clients are more likely to talk to you when you start your own business.

I wouldn't advise just handing in your notice on Friday and starting your own business on the following Monday as you need to give yourself a window of time to enable you to get everything set-up and get yourself into that position. I would advise a minimum of six months of planning and setting up. If you do get work in, in the meantime, don' just jump at it, you could either sub contract it out to somebody you trust or turn it down. I know this may seem a little strange, but believe me, you are better turning the work down than giving your current job up for a promise of two weeks work and nothing for two months after that. You need to make sure you have a steady stream of enquiries, coming in and that you are being competitive in the market place to enable you to make the judgment on when you take the step. You will also get an instinctive feeling when to go for it.

I would advise having a minimum of six months money in your personal account to cover your outgoings when you do go for it. You want to minimise as much financial pressure as you can when first starting out, the last thing you want is to be worrying about paying your mortgage when you are trying to get your business up and running.

So, let's look at your start-up costs:

- Company registration both UK and United States – anything up to £130.00 or $220.00 dollars – One off cost.
- Insurance – Public Liability & Employers Liability if you employ operatives – My first years insurance for an electrical contracting business was £337.13 ($572.77 USD) based on £10,000 ($16,989.63 USD) cover for Employers Liability and £5,000 ($8,494.81 USD) for Public Liability – this was based on a first year turnover of £75,000 ($127,422.29 USD) You may also need to take out PI (Professional Indemnity) Insurance if there is part of your work that involves you designing the items you will be installing I.E. If you are a plumber and you are calculating the size of pipework you are installing then this becomes a design element. My cost for PI for the first year was: £130.00 ($220.86 USD) – These costs are annually.
- Office - I would advise working from home initially if you can. If you are renting an office, you will pay by square foot and also be aware of any service charge you may have.
- Phones – I would advise having a mobile phone and also a landline number, which you can generally get as one package for around £40 ($67.95 USD) per month.
- Set-up a website hosting account – £20 ($33.97 USD) per month
- Set-up a website - £500 ($847.47 USD)

Example Start-up Cost Spreadsheet

Start Up Costs	Balance
Opening Balance - investment	1,700.00 ($*2881.40 USD)
Company House – State Registration	130.00 ($ 220.86 USD)
Standard Insurance	337.13 ($ 572.77 USD)
Specialist Insurance - PI	130.00 ($ 220.86 USD)
Office IT Expenditure - PC	
Mobile Phone / Landline	40.00 ($67.95 USD)
Office Phone – If Required	
Office Rent – If Required	
Office Bills (Service Charge)	
Office Equipment	
Plant Steps - Drills etc.	
Vehicle & Insurance	
Website	£500.00 ($847.47)
Stationary – Letter heads etc.	220.00 ($ 373.77 USD)
Workware	100.00 ($169.89 USD)
E-Mail & Web Hosting	20.00 ($ 33.97 USD)
Advertising	200.00 ($ 339.79 USD)
Wages	0.00
Vat Account	
Total	1,677.13 ($2842.64)

As you can see above, I have put an investment into the company initially of £1,700 or ($2881.40 USD), You can then determine what other costs you need to add that will be applicable to your business to get you started. I have put the very basic items on here that you need, assuming you already have things like a computer, vehicle and tools to enable you to carry out the work. Whatever you do not have, you will need to factor in.

Your "**to do**" list of setting your company up:

- Decide on your company name – read previous chapter on this before choosing your name.
- Decide what type of company you want to operate – I.E. sole trader/ limited. – Read previous chapter on types of companies.
- Register your company with Companies House or file information on your department for state's home page.
- Open a bank account – never pay for an account. I would also suggest getting an account that enables you to carry out internet banking as this is the easiest method these days. Note, some banks will charge you to use a cheque, so use them sparingly.
- Get the company insured – I would suggest using specialist trade insurance companies as these will tend to be more specific to your industry and will tend to cover you for more.

- Register for VAT if required (Not in USA) – This is not a requirement if you trade under £79,000($134,218.15 USD) per year. Please read previous chapter on VAT before deciding on registering for it.
- Decide where you will be working from; home, rented office, virtual office.
- Get your internet sorted, just type domain hosting into Google and you will get several internet companies that will offer you a monthly subscription. The minimum you receive in your package is a free domain name, and at least 10 e-mail addresses with the account. This should cost less than £5.00 or $8.00 per month.
- Get your domain name registered for your company, so if you are called Hills Plumbing, then you need to try and get a Domain name as close to this as possible, such as www.hillsplumbing.com or something similar if this is not available.
- Sort your phones out. I would always get a landline and mobile number. A lot of mobile phone providers offer a landline number with your mobile phone. The landline number will then transfer any calls to your mobile. It always looks better if you have a landline number printed on your documents, it makes you look like you are established in one place.
- Once you have your address, brand name/logo, domain name and phone numbers, you are ready to get your stationary designed and ordered. I would advise

obtaining the following as a minimum; business cards, letter headed paper and compliment slips. Search the internet and you will find many print companies out there. One crucial bit of advice, don't go for cheap business cards, spend a little more on these as you want your card to be exciting and want your customer to remember it and not chuck it to the back of the draw. I suggest having the following items on the card:

1. A Picture of You
2. Your Business Name / brand / Logo
3. Your business Address and website
4. Contact numbers
5. Testimonial
6. Your name
7. Your position
8. Any trade association you are registered with
9. A brief explanation of what you do, so for example; Painting and Decorating Guru's and a slogan like; "We make your home something your friends talk about"

Always use a good quality cardstock to get them printed on. There are many types of cardstock out there such as spot varnished or embossed, remember don't go cheap on these.

Same with your letter heads, use a good quality paper, and make sure the page is designed so that you can use it in the entire document you send as some companies will have a main heading page and then continuation pages with less information on. Top tip, before placing the order with your printer, make sure they will send you a copy of your stationary in a word document so that you can use it on your computer which enables you to send the documents by e-mail instead of hard copy in the post.

Get a website up and running. You need to be careful here. If you get what is called a fully coded website, then generally only a website designer will be able to modify it, which will have an associated cost with it each time you make a change. There are many platforms out there to host your website. One that is commonly used is called WordPress. WordPress can be altered by you without too much technical knowledge. Your website also needs to be what is called mobile friendly, which means that it can be viewed on all smart devices such as phones and tablets. I will talk more about websites in the marketing section of this book.

Ge an accountant. Managing your money, I would advise against trying to manage your money yourself. I tried this at first and it just takes up to much of your time that you should be spending on your business. I guarantee it will take you at least three times as long as it does a bookkeeper or an accountant. You can outsource your accounts as many accountants and bookkeepers will work on an hourly basis for you. To give you an idea, one of my business currently turns over around £1M ($1,698,963.97 USD) per year and the accountant charges me £360 ($611.62 USD) per month for their services. It saves me a lot of time and I also know that my accounts have been done correctly. You can get a good bookkeeper for around £11.77 ($20.00 USD) per hour. If you look on the internet and Google search accountants/bookkeepers you will find somebody that will do it. There is one note to take here though, I would always use an accountant that is in proximity of your place of work as there are times where you need to go and see them face to face.

Cash flow & Finances - Cash flow should always be at the forefront of any business and should be monitored constantly. People can get mixed up between cash flow and profit and loss accounts. Your cash flow is a reflection of money coming in and going out in your business and gives you a true value of your cash in your business. Profit and loss sheets advise you the amount you have invoiced out to your customers by accruals and the money you have paid out to your suppliers etc. This is where some people get confused as they think cash flow and profit and loss are the same, which they are not, so for example, I will use a company that makes widgets and each one is £3.00 ($5.09 USD) to buy from me. The cost of the widgets for me to make or buy is £1.50($2.54. USD), therefore I essentially make £1.50 ($2.54. USD) for each one I sell.

Let's say I have sold 200 of these widgets to a customer who I allow to pay on 30 day terms (which means they pay 30 days after

they have received them) so the cost to the customer = £3.00 ($5.09 USD) x 200 = £600.00 ($1019.37 USD)
Let's say I have to pay my supplier straight away, therefore I have paid them £1.50 ($2.54. USD) x 200 = £300.00 ($509.68 USD)

Now my profit and loss sheet would say that I have invoiced £600.00($1019.37 USD) from the customers and paid £300.00 ($509.68 USD) to my supplier giving me a profit of £300.00 ($509.68 USD) Net.

My cash flow would say I am at a loss of £300.00 ($509.68 USD) until I get paid for the widgets after the 30 days. Therefore you need to factor in your outgoing costs in that 30 day period until you get paid and then typically you very rarely get paid on time so you may end up waiting 45 to 60 days or even longer which can restrict cash in your business and this can cause you a major problem.

Invoicing & Getting Paid – This can be one of your biggest headaches. You need to have a system in place for invoicing which helps with your cash flow, I would suggest always allocating yourself a set time once a week to go through your invoicing and get it done. Don't put it off, you need to get money in as your suppliers will be invoicing you and as per the section on cash flow, you need to have money coming in to pay the bills going out.

If you are working for domestic customers, expect to be paid on completion of the work. It would also be advisable on getting a deposit upfront to at least cover your materials

If you are working for businesses then expect to have credit terms set up by them where you will be paid after 30 days. Some businesses try and pay you after 90 days which ends up being 120 days. To be honest I would steer clear of anybody that doesn't pay within 45 days. You will find that construction companies are one of the worst, business sectors having exceptionally long payment dates and then they will argue how much they will pay you. You need to have your paper work up to scratch to make sure you get paid on time and for the correct amount. Keep records of everything you do including your time on site and your supplies that you have purchased for proof if necessary.

I would always advise following up with an e-mail or phone call about a week before payment is due to remind them, it is surprising how many people forget they need to pay you.

One of the biggest mistakes I have made personally in business is being too trusting and assuming that all people are decent and pay their bills. Don't make the same mistake as me as it will cost you money, it cost me to the tune of £30,000 ($50,968.91) in 2013 with 3 customers not paying me. Yes you can take legal action but you need to have all correspondence to back everything up and sometimes the cost of using a solicitor and the time and stress it gives you to get your money back far outweighs the money that is unpaid. A lot of people know that it costs you money to chase payment, so they will hold payment on purpose. I have a business acquaintance that I know will wait to the very last moment to pay as on several occasions the company they owe money too has gone into administration and he has got away without paying them anything and pocketing the money himself. Unethical I know, but people out there do this and they will do it to you if they can get away with it.

Keep on top of your invoicing and make sure the correct information is on the invoice, try and send via e-mail with a message receipt or if by post get it recorded delivery, you will always come across customers that say they haven't received the bill.

Summary of Chapter 5

Be aware of the initial startup costs of owning your own business. Be sure the costs are manageable before you make the jump and that you follow the checklist provided or refer to Tradesman-Academy.com. You will average at least £1,700 ($2881.40 USD) in initial startup costs which include Company House – State Registration, insurance, office materials and supplies, phones both mobile and landline, office equipment, plant steps and equipment drills etc., and vehicles.

Many other business decisions must be made or done such as:

- Your company name
- Type of business structure
- Registration with Companies House
- Open a bank account
- Get your domain name registered
- Insure your company
- Register for VAT if required
- Decide where you will be working from
- Build a website
- Hire an accountant

You'll need business cards, a website, accounts and procedures for cash flow and for getting paid.

When deciding when and how to go it on your own don't go after clients that the company you are employed by as it is unethical and can also get you into problems legally. Also, I wouldn't advise handing in your notice on Friday and starting your own business on the following Monday. You need to give yourself a window of time to enable you to get everything set-up and get yourself into that position. I would advise a minimum of six months of planning and setting up.

I would advise having a minimum of six months money in your personal account to cover your outgoings when you do go for it. You want to minimise as much financial pressure as you can when first starting out.

CHAPTER 6

MARKETING

I believe there are three key areas that should be the priority in any business; 1) Marketing 2), Cash flow, and 3) The service you provide your customers.

Without marketing you will not get any customers, and without any customers you do not have a business. Cash flow we will talk about in another chapter, so let's get on with marketing.

Before you start any marketing you need to figure out who you will be marketing to and also do your numbers;

You may have heard of the three M's

M - Market

M – Message

M- Media

Okay, we start with the Market. These will be your customers. Now let's take a look at one of my businesses, Eviva Services – which is an electrical installation and contracting business. Now I have an option here, my market could be one of three following or possibly a combination of all, however you do need to niche down to a specific target market as your Message and types of Media will be determined by this.

The three markets I have:
1) Domestic customer – those who own their own homes or rent properties out.
2) Commercial Customer – businesses such as supermarkets, public buildings such as libraries, schools, or office blocks.
3) Industrial Customer – Larger factories, and Heavy industry.

Now, each of these I would target my M, M & M differently for. I tend to focus on the commercial and industrial customers purely because they give me a higher profit margin to the business and it is the work I prefer doing. I would say less than 10% of my business is for the domestic customer.

What I am going to explain to you now is really important! You need to determine who your main target market is because this will dictate how you market to them

Domestic Customers and Commercial & Industrial Customers:

Split testing is how you test different marketing methods to tell what offers and marketing customers respond to. Don't just rely on one type of marketing either, you need to use different methods and what is known as split testing which I will talk about shortly

It's so important to do – it's how you find out what offers and approaches your audience responds to.

There are several methods of marketing out there that I am going list

- Website
- PPC - Google AdWords
- Re-marketing
- SEO – Search Engine Optimisation
- E-mail Marketing
- Telesales
- Direct Mail
- Social Media – Facebook / Twitter / LinkedIn
- Newsletters
- Webinars / how to - YouTube
- Joint Venture
- Newspapers / Press Ads
- Referrals
- Leaflets / Post Cards
- Local Directories
- Third Party Website enquires
- Networking such as BNI groups
- Google Maps which is free and easy to set-up

Website - Your website will be a critical part of your business, you need to have the correct design to engage with the customers you want, for example, I have a website designed for the commercial and industrial customers rather than the domestic customers. I still get enquiries from domestic, however they are very limited. Obviously, if you intend to obtain domestic customers then your website will be designed with Domestic customers in mind.

Your website must contain certain information and have the correct layout as you need to have contact numbers in the right places and also have a lead capture form on the website, again in the right place. You need at least three call to action points on each page of your website. We talk more about this in Tradesman Academy.

When you build your website make sure you include:
* The benefits of doing work with your business
* Show some before and after pictures
* Include customer testimony
* Have a signup form for information
* Provide a "tips and advice section"

PPC - Google AdWords – Google AdWords are a primary driver in internet marketing. AdWords can help you get the right message to the customers you want to reach by using the specific keywords that will lead them to your business. AdWords can be unique for each type of business you do such as plumbing and air conditioning. You may run one ad for plumbing and one for air conditioning

although your company provides both services. AdWords allows you to use geo-targeting to reach customers in your particular area. You can focus your ads to specific devices, times of the day, or days of the week.

PPC – Pay Per Click - Google AdWords is in my top three methods of getting customers interested. PPC works via searching the internet for a product or service, so for example, if you went onto the search engine Google and typed in Electrical Contractors, then the following would appear on the page:

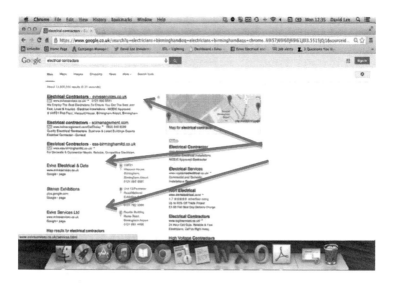

You can see on the page above that my company; Eviva Services appears on the first page of Google 3 times. Once in the very first ad at the top and then twice in the Google Places section below. There is a lot to understand about Google AdWords and we cover this in the Academy. You can get a lot of companies that will contact you and guarantee you a first page listing on Google for so much money a month. Be careful if you choose this route as it can be expensive and these companies will guarantee you certain keywords (which will be explained in the Academy) however the keywords they give you will generally always be what are called long tail keywords. Let me explain a long tail keyword. "An electrician with a pair of pliers in north Wisconsin" If you type this in will give you a top place ad. Unfortunately the likelihood of this being typed in by an internet searcher is very minute so be careful. Also your ads make a massive difference on conversions, I will show you two examples of adds below for the same thing. One had a CTR of 0.1% and the other a CTR of 3.6%. CTR is a Click Through Rate. The CTR shows basically how many people clicked through after searching for a service or product similar to your keyword. Anything above a 2% click through rate is good on Google, which basically means for every 100 customers that search for a keyword, at least two clicks went through to your site. The job is not over yet. Strategic keyword selection is needed to rank your site high corresponding to what the average internet searcher may enter. Your website needs to be able to engage the customer and get information from them.

To run ads, you have to bid on them to position yourself on the page, so for example you may bid $1 to be on the first page, but if a competitor bids $1.20 then they could be placed above you, however without complicating things for the purpose of this Book, your page ranking is also taken into account which is related to your content on your site and how relevant it is to your customer.

Example of CTR – Click Through Rate – Information from the Adwords Guru, Perry Marshall

The difference can be quite amazing. Here's an example of two ads – they are ALMOST IDENTICAL but one got nearly TWENTY TIMES the CTR as the other:

Popular Ethernet Terms	**Popular Ethernet Terms**
3 Page Guide – Free PDF Download	Complex Words – Simple Definitions
Complex Words – Simple Definitions	3 Page Guide – Free PDF Download
www.bb-elec.com	www.bb-elec.com
2 Clicks – CTR 0.1%	39 Clicks – CTR 3.6%

Notice what happened: All I did was reverse two lines – and the clickthrough rate jumped from 0.1% to 3.6%!

The above is also a great example of what marketers call split testing. For example, if you have 100 prospects you wish to send direct mail, e-mail, post cards or on Google AdWords, always split test them. What does this mean? Let's say I am sending out 100 direct mail letters, I would give half a different subject heading and write them slightly different to see which had the most take up. You then do this again on your next direct mail campaign with a different subject line and compare against the one that worked better last time. Therefore you are always testing what works and what doesn't. This is the same principle for the Google Ads. The Ads were written for the same product, yet you can see one far out beats the other.

Re-marketing - We have all seen the sign for "Allow Cookies" on websites when we are searching for various things on the internet. Basically this enables the site with the Cookie on it to follow you around with ads for so-many days thereafter, typically around 60 days. The cookie attaches itself to your searches and when you look on other websites you will see ads appear on the page advertising something from a site that you have previously been on in the last 60 days which encourages you to go back to the site. This is known as re-targeting.

SEO – Search Engine Optimisation - You will hear a lot of people talking about SEO. Why is it important? You have two ways to get to the first page of Google, the first is as per the PPC AdWords as mentioned previously where you pay and bid to be on the page. The second is by Organic Search which is how Google Ranks you regarding the content you put on your website and how relevant it is to your customers which is where SEO comes in. The more SEO you do with quality content the higher Google will rank you, so even if somebody is bidding $2.00 on AdWords and you are

69

bidding $0.60 but you are constantly updating relevant content on your site, you are likely to rank above your competitor.

Does it matter where you are placed on the first page of Google? Yes, I believe it does, if my ads are not shown in certain areas of the screen then I tend to get less Click Through.

This is both a science and an art that is simplified in Tradesman-Academy. The Internet is one of the major players in marketing and advertising today. If a customer needs to hire a trade this is where they go. If I want to expand a pub and need lighting, plumbing, and electrical, where am I going to search? The Internet.

E-mail Marketing - E-mail marketing is another source of getting customers, however this can be hit and miss. The thing here is to have a good list of people to e-mail to. There are many companies out there that sell lists and these are easily found on the Internet, just be careful, as some of the information can be very old. You also need to think about who you are targeting, if you only want to reach people within a 30 mile radius of where you work there is no point in getting e-mail addresses for people outside of this geographical area.

Telesales - Effectively this is another word for cold calling people. I wouldn't recommend using this if you are targeting domestic customers. It has worked for me for commercial and industrial customers, you can either do this yourself or get a company to do it for you. If you are good on the phone do it yourself as nobody knows your business like you do. If you are not so confident, then outsource, there are plenty of companies that do it for you. I would always choose two companies and then give them a 100 calls each to make and see who provides you the best outcome for your business.

Direct Mail - This is one of my favorites and does well due to the fact that most people receive e-mails, text messages etc. these days, less direct mail is sent, so people are more intrigued to find out what is in it. The important thing here is to get your mail to stand out, I use bright green envelopes for a start, you then need to have good subject headlines and have good copy to get people to take action. This can be a very good way of marketing if done correctly.

Social Media - We are all aware of the social media sites out there, such as Facebook, Twitter, LinkedIn, Google+ etc., there will be many more coming our way in the future, and it is advisable to get a presence on social media, even if you only do it a couple of times a week, it will help in other parts of your business such as your SEO.

Newsletters - Newsletters are a great way of communicating with existing customers, I know people that do these monthly and others that do it every quarter. I would suggest not doing this until you have started to build your customer base. Newsletters are good to keep you in customer's minds and that is where you need to be. They might not be ready to buy from you there and then, but when they are, you need to be their first thought.

Webinars / How To? and YouTube - Publishing what you do on YouTube is a great way of getting customers. Link the Video to Your website, and the added bonus you have is guess what!!!! Google owns YouTube so it can only be a good thing for your search optimisation. The key here is to do short videos, no more than 5 minutes long, ideally 3 minutes and show the customer how to do something. For example a plumber might show you how to change a radiator valve. Keep building the collection of video's and guess what? Every time someone has a plumbing problem, where do they go first? Your video and your website.

Joint Venture or JV's as some people call them - If you are a local painter and decorator, talk to local electricians and plumbers, to see if they will recommend you to their clients and you offer to do the same for them. Also, go into your local shops such as Barbour's and offer something like a free coat of paint to the seating area every year if they allow you to put an advertisement in their shop for your company and recommend your company.

Newspapers / Press Ads - You can advertise in newspapers fairly cheaply at this time as most are struggling with the constant fight against the internet, the key to newspaper ads is to get a great subject line to entice customers, Don't go for 10% of this week, everybody does this, you need to offer more. You can get free advertising by doing something in the community and getting the press to cover it. This will put you ahead of your competition.

Referrals - Referrals are a big source of work for my businesses; a large amount of work that comes in to my electrical business is from referrals. You need to make sure you do a fantastic job for the customer. Get them to fill in a testimonial that you can use for future customers as this supports your credibility in your business. You can offer them an incentive if they refer you to one of their friends and they also have work done. Make sure you offer both people the incentive, as this will work better for you. After you have finished re-wiring a customer's house, send a gift such as a bunch of flowers to Mrs. Williams or a set of golf balls with his name on them to Mr. Williams and a note, saying, "Hope we didn't cause you too much disruption and hope we didn't cause to much mess, by the way the tea was lovely." Mr. & Mrs. Williams will always recommend you to their friends or colleagues as long as you have carried out a great job because you are different. Yes it has cost you a bunch of flowers, but add that onto the cost of the next house re-wire you get from her friend. (Just be careful in case her husband takes offence at the flowers!!!!!)

Leaflets / Post Cards - Another method of direct marketing, always make sure you use both sides of the leaflet or postcard. You generally have the time it takes the client to walk from the front door to the bin in their kitchen to get their attention so make sure your headline is good. A wise move for dropping leaflets or postcards is to drop them in the area that you are currently working on a house as you can sometimes get the Smith and Jones effect. So if you're a decorator working in house number 37 on the street, then Mrs. Jenkins that lives at No 41 will possibly want her house decorating also as we wouldn't want number 37 having a better looking house than number 41 would we!

You may also want to ask if you can display a sign advertising your company and its services on the project you are working on. Yard signs are a great form of advertising while you perform work. Such as "Halliday Construction Company". "Call For A Quote And Speak To Dean"

Local Directories - Local directories can be good for business leads, but you have to be careful when selecting these. Look for different types of directories in your local area such as parish magazines, or similar, we have a local one called "Look Local". Take a look at other competitors advertising in your local area and see if they are in there regularly. If they are then this tends to show it is working for them, again to stand out from the rest you need to make your message better and more prominent than everybody else's and testimonials of other customers help.

Third Party Website enquires - There are companies out there who advertise on the Internet such as Rated People, Check a Trade, or Trust a Trader. I have used these in the past and it can be a good source of work if you are in the domestic market. They work by getting at least four companies to quote for the same job and you find that people will tend to go for the cheapest quote. You have to pay for each lead you get which can be expensive at times as the price has gone up significantly since these companies started out. I would only use this as a back-up to my main marketing.

Call Tracking - I think this is a must in business as you need to track where you are getting your work from and then concentrate on making the most of them. So for example you are using 4 of the methods mentioned above for your marketing:

1) – Website
2) – Direct Mail Letter
3) – Postcard / Leaflet
4) – Local Directories

With each one of these I would have a tracking number, which is a specific landline phone number for each piece of marketing so you will have a phone number on your website, your direct mail letter etc. These cost very little, around £3.00 GBP ($5.00 USD) per month and you will have a weekly list sent to you showing who made the call, which number has been called, (identifying which marketing is working the best) how long the call was, and if you have missed any calls, which you don't want as this may be missed customers.

Remember, the purpose of marketing is to get a lifetime customer, play the long game, you need to keep regular contact with people as they are not always ready to buy when you initially contact them, however you need to be at the forefront of their mind when they do need you.

The cost of acquiring customers – Do your numbers, the purpose of getting a sale is to get a customer. You need to know and understand these numbers before you can start working out how much you'd be prepared to spend on getting a new customer.

For example, you see if a new customer is worth £58.85 ($100 USD) to you within 30 days (Let's say you're selling low end Fridge's) but repeat business isn't typical, then a customer's lifetime value isn't going to be much higher than that, so what would you pay to get a new customer worth £58.85 ($100 USD) to you? £5.88 ($10 USD)? £17.65 ($30 USD)? Not much more than that I suspect.

Let's say we're a plumbing company and your customer asks you to carry out maintenance every month and spends £147.14 ($250 USD) per month to have the work carried out. The lifetime value is MUCH higher and is likely to run into thousands. In this scenario, the amount you pay will be much higher than with the Fridge business. You might spend a lot more than your initial $250 amount of money that you make from the first month, which is not uncommon in what is called aggressive marketing and is called going under water.

Once you know and understand how much a customer is worth to you, then you can start thinking about how much you'd be prepared to spend to get a customer. As long as you do your numbers, and your numbers are solid, then my advice would be to be prepared to spend as much as you can afford to.

Here's Why:

Cut Through the Clutter

Think about how many e-mail's your prospective customer gets in a day? How many do they put straight into the trash folder, which gets ignored?

How likely is your prospect to ignore a 4ft box tied up with ribbon, with their name on it?

Every business is trying to get customers by spending very little money. Think of all that marketing, all those same sales letters and quarter-page adverts, which are easy to miss or ignore.

Up your game and spend a little to get the right customer and you can cut through that clutter and get your business noticed. Most businesses spend a bare minimum, so the bar isn't set high enough. When was the last time any business sent you a gift of any kind or anything out of the ordinary or memorable?

Spend More to Get a Better Customer

These are some key customer base concepts to keep in mind.

- Cheap customers buy on price
- Cheap customers are typically more demanding
- Cheap customers will cause you more problems.
- Think, less customers spending more money is better than more customers spending little money and you do less work.

People ask me how to advertise and market their business for little or no cost. Well the reality is, if you want your business to grow and make you more money, you cannot, not spend money and time in advertising and get results. It takes money to make money.

CRM – Customer Relationship Management - A CRM is a key building block in any business and I believe all businesses need one. There is one business owner that I know who I quote "I would rather have my electricity cut off and use a generator than lose my CRM" This business has around 6,000 people on their CRM system.

So what is a CRM and how does it work?

A CRM works by collecting information from prospects by obtaining their names, e-mail addresses and other information. An example of this is a sign up form on a website which is linked to a CRM.

Depending on how advanced your CRM is, the system will automatically send out information to people who are signed up on your list via a web form or some other form of list. So for example, your company has an offer this month on a service to gas boilers where you are doing it for half price. With the CRM you type one e-mail and you can send this information to your list on the CRM. Your list may have 250 people on it. In particular they are the customers you have built up by getting an e-mail address after you have installed a boiler in their house, so you know when their boiler is due for a service.

I know one person who has a florist and uses a CRM to target customers by sending a message out a week before a signed up persons birthday to see if they want a bunch of flowers sent. You see, when the person first got their customer, they asked certain questions such as the date of birth of their wife/husband, mom etc., and therefore this information can be used in a CRM to run automatically and to help matters when the person bought their initial bunch of flowers they took their credit card details, so now this makes it even easier for the florist, all she needs to do is get the customer to confirm they want the flowers and they already have all the information they need to process the sale.

What does CRM cost? It depends on who you go with, but costs start from around £11.00 ($18.64 USD) per month. I personally use Aweber which works for me, there are several in the market place to choose from, each offering different solutions.

Your Image - Your image is very important and you generally only get one chance at this as most people's minds are made up about you before you even speak. If you turn up to a customer looking scruffy then don't expect to get the work. Even your company vehicle needs to look the part. If your van is dirty then the prospect will generally have the impression that you will carry out your work in an untidy and messy fashion. Have a professional look.

- Wear a company uniform even if it is just you. You can get yourself fully kitted out with Logo's on your clothes for less than $100 and this will pay dividends in the long run.
- Respect people's property. When you go to somebodies property, do small things like wear overshoes over your boots when you enter the property, and don't smoke or eat in front of people. If this is necessary, do so in your truck or van.
- Don't swear and always ask politely if you can use their facilities, don't assume you can!

Summary of chapter 6

Marketing is the single most important activity that will contribute to your company's success and the reason behind such a lengthy chapter.

I believe there are three key areas that should be the priority in any business; 1) Marketing 2), Cash flow, and 3) The service you provide your customers.

Marketing has multiple approaches and it includes management of your website, Google AdWords, SEO – Search Engine Optimisation, E-mail Marketing, Telesales, Direct Mail, and Social Media – Facebook / Twitter / LinkedIn.

Your company's image is at stake and it is your responsibility to promote it positively to build your business, whether this is a website presence, your uniform, business cards, or vehicle wrap promoting your business.

Remember the 3'M's Market, Message, and Media used for the three markets I have:
1) Domestic customer – those who own their own homes or rent properties out
2) Commercial Customer – businesses such as supermarkets, public buildings such as libraries, schools, or office blocks.
3) Industrial Customer – Larger factories, and Heavy industry.

Each of these are targeted differently and I tend to focus on the commercial and industrial customers purely because they give me a higher profit margin to the business and it is the work I prefer doing.

You should spend more to get a better customer and remember that

- Cheap customers buy on price
- Cheap customers are typically more demanding
- Cheap customers will cause you more problems.
- Less customers spending more money is better than more customers spending little money and you do less work.

Customer Relationship Management is a key building block in any business and you need one. A CRM system will automatically send out information to people who are signed up on your email list via a web form or some other form of list.

The key to getting to your customer is to cut through the clutter and use a multiple system marketing approach.

Always use more than one method of marketing, don't just hope for the best by using one.

Don't forget your professional image. This includes each piece of your business the customer can see; your business card, uniform, vehicle, clean tools, and swearing on the job down to your logo on your invoices. All aspects of your business need to reflect professionalism.

CHAPTER 7

OUTSOURCING & EMPLOYING PEOPLE

I see a lot of tradesmen who don't grow their business purely because they are worried about taking somebody on. They might stretch to having an apprentice or laborer to help them on a daily basis or when the work calls for it, however some people do seem afraid of the commitment of taking somebody on. They feel that they may lose control of some of the business or that because they are not personally doing the job it will not be to their standard. This is fine as long as you never want to grow your business. Your business will never change unless you help it too. I have several employees working for me and I would be lying if I said it was easy and at times they can be frustrating. If you want to grow you will need to free up your time. This will require you to take staff on temporarily or permanently and the best way to do this is by damage limitation and careful selection.

The first thing I would advise is to outsource what parts of your business you can, i.e use a bookkeeper for so many hours per week or a personal assistant for so many hours per week dependent on your tasks. I outsource a lot of my administrative work and it works well for me. Outsourced employees are generally on an hourly rate or per task/job rate and if you are not happy with them, then it is easy to change to somebody else, by doing this, it reduces your commitment.

If you are looking at taking somebody on direct, make sure you have a standard form of contract written which you issue to them and get them to sign. Make sure their hourly rate is defined in the contract as well as their holiday entitlements and bank holidays including what happens when they need to take doctors' appointments etc. as this can cause problems after you employ them. I would also never take anybody on as a salary paid job where they get paid should they be off work or ill. All my staff are hourly paid and receive no sick pay from me, only what they are entitled to from the government or state. This may sound like I am tight, but I very rarely have people off sick and if they are I know they are sick. It is always at your discretion if you wish to pay them thereafter. I personally know several people who wouldn't think twice about having time off sick purely because they are salaried and are getting paid. I also know if they weren't getting paid, they would not have 1/10 of the time they have off as sick.

Make sure you interview people, you do have to be careful here and I would always ask a HR company for advice on interviews as you have to make sure you are asking the same questions to each candidate and also being fair to each candidate. Remember it's your choice in the end.

A little advice, I have interviewed people that have come across brilliantly in the interview answering all questions with the right answers and their CV has looked really good. Don't let this fool you, I have been caught out twice with this scenario, thinking I was taking on somebody that I thought was perfect for the job and in the end have turned out to be completely the opposite.

I look for three things when I look for a new employee.

1) Try and establish how keen they are on actually getting a job. There are many people out there who get an interview just so as they don't lose their employment benefits and don't really want the job, it is just an exercise for this type of person and will be a waste of your time.

2) Without doubt, I will always favour someone that has actually gone out and got themselves educated by paying for their own higher education such as night courses at college etc. as if they are willing to do this they are willing to work.

3) Common sense. I would always ask what I call common sense questions in an interview and the answers they give would stand the better ones out from the rest. Although specific training is needed for most jobs especially a trade skill, this can generally be taught. However common sense is definitely one of the main

factors I believe in an employee. If they have this then I believe you can teach them anything else.

One of my businesses is an electrical contracting company. Now I would always employ a 16 year old apprentice with average grades and common sense than a 19 year old apprentice that has been in the industry for 3 years that come across as having no common sense. The other advantage of having somebody that isn't trained yet is that you can train them to meet your expectations.

There are times when you need to take skilled people on and I find that the better ones will always be actively employed in work and only tend to jump to another company for three reasons. 1) The money is better. 2) Where they are working is closer to home. 3) They are able to climb the ladder by moving to another company.

A word about agencies; I am not a fan of agencies, and I will probably be ridiculed for saying this but 80% of agency employees are at an agency because they are not reliable as far as work ethic, reliability, competency, or skill basically, because they are not great at their profession. From my experience I would say that for every 10-agency operatives I have employed, only 1 will be any good.

Outsourcing & Employing People - Outsourcing for your company may come in several different forms. You may outsource work on your Internet website for expertise in Search Engine

Optimization (SEO), you may outsource administrative office work through a virtual assistant or bookkeeping through an online service. You may also employ subcontractors to complete the many components of a construction project you have including concrete, painting, electrical, plumbing, architecture, interior design etc.

Here are some additional key tips and best practices for outsourcing and employing people for all categories. Following this information are the specifics to look out for specific outsourced categories.

1. To begin, clearly define the scope and schedule for your project.

To receive the best quality service it is important to clearly convey in a statement or scope of work your expected goals for a project. This lets the contractor know the job requirements, expectations, and deliverables and allows them in return to provide you with a more concise bid for your work. Your timelines for project deliverables are important at this stage as the longer a project takes the longer it is for money to enter your pockets. This is the same as setting your expectations and priorities.

2. Determine frequency of communications.

Always ensure once the individual is hired they have frequent communication with you based on your requirements. What types of status updates do you want? How often? What are the problems? What is going well? How is the project schedule progressing?

3. Set escalation parameters

What do you want to be notified about and what types of issues require your notification and intervention? Remember this is a time management function for you. You don't need to be overwhelmed with the small details. Your time is best spent focusing on opportunities. Here's an example: In order to free up my time with unnecessary calls from virtual assistants or my contracted tradesman I give them a degree of levity with operations. For the virtual administrative employees I empower them to make corrective actions and customer service recovery. If a customer is complaining about a replacement of a 20A breaker or a smudge on carpet I allow my employee to correct it on the spot if the action is below a threshold of say £70 or $120 USD. This does two things; It frees up my time and provides excellent customer satisfaction and/or customer retention. My customers know I value them and my employees know they have the power to boost my business to the next level as it will be known for customer satisfaction.

4. Begin on a small scale

When you're working with a contractor, whether it be a tradesman or an administrative position start out with a small project which is minimal in scope. This will give you an opportunity to see the contractor's capabilities quality and timeliness towards the project.

5. Payment

Use payments as leverage towards the completion of jobs. This is a concept that is used whether the individual is new or a contractor you have been using for quite some time. Always tie your payments to specific milestones for the project. This way your deadlines and quality standards are met prior to payment. Minimize any upfront payments, pay as you go, and hold 20 to 30% of the project cost until the final deliverable is completed or milestone is met.

6. Price selection

When selecting by price make sure that your choice in contractor represents the best value for your company in terms of quality and cost. It is often a good idea to discard the highest price and also the lowest price bidders, unless there is some substantial reason for choosing the highest bidder or lowest bidder or if you simply don't care about quality.

7. Legal requirements

Be aware of legal requirements when negotiating a contract or virtual work. Any type of project that you outsource may require an understanding of the content ownership. Are you going to require a nondisclosure agreement? Are you going to require complete ownership of the final work? Are you negotiating copyrighted material? Be sure this is included in the negotiation of the contract.

8. Warranty work

Warranty work is another issue to consider when working with a freelancer, outsourced person, or contractor. It is important to know what type of support or warranty is offered in terms of the final service. If this is not negotiated in the original contract you may need to hire an additional contractor to complete work which should have been included in the original project.

9. Contract in writing

Make sure all of the requirements for a project or service are obtained in writing. This should include the scope of the project and the deliverables, the milestones, the price, modifications, and communications expectations. Remember you're the owner of the company and your success hinges on acquiring the best contracted employees.

10. Review potential contractors as if you were hiring a full time employee

Another good rule of thumb to use when acquiring outsourced employees when you are evaluating proposals is to review the contractors as if you were interviewing for a full-time employee that will be with your company for many years. Make sure you get feedback, do a portfolio review, and ask specific questions related to your project. Make sure that the contractor is responsive to your issues and concerns.

As you hire more contractors, subcontractors, freelancers, and outsourced personnel the selection process should become easier. You will be more familiar with the questions to ask in the evaluation of bids and how to weed out incompetent outsourced personnel.

In summary, these are the key points to be aware of for outsourced work. One is to make sure that you hold strong with deadlines for task completion. This will also include the quality of work in relation to your deadlines. Next, make sure that you maintain routine communication. Hold the contractor or outsourced personnel accountable for what they do and to make sure they are on task. Finally, you may want to use additional structured payment program which is also called a layered approach. In the layered approach you incentivize the contractor to do additional work by providing additional tasks which if completed will be compensated in addition to the contracted base amount.

11. In order to be sure you have the best contracted tradesman or construction contractors there are several aspects you should be aware of.

These include:

- Review of the contractor's license & qualifications
- Checking to see if they are insured and what it covers
- Doing a background check and criminal record check
- Checking references

Here is some of the reasoning on why you need to perform some of these actions. First of all they will eliminate a lot of headaches by hiring the right person who is competent as a tradesman, honest, and with a minimal historical risk for failure.

I think it's fairly safe to say or understand at this point in the book that you can see the value in not hiring the wrong person. Hiring an unlicensed or incompetent individual will result in inferior work, rework, additional cost, and possibly court disputes to settle disagreements on work performed. All of these are issues which will cost you money.

12. Checking the contractor's license. Checking the contractor's license can be accomplished through several means. You may be able to search with the Better Business Bureau in the US or inquire records through the local construction permitting agency to provide information on customer or contract complaints filed against a contractor or their license. They may have details on mechanical liens which may be held for incomplete or improper work. You may also be able to use these to tell if the contractor is licensed for their trade and whether they carry liability insurance for accidents and injuries or are bonded for even higher cost projects.

13. Contract design. The next step is to make sure you have a rock-solid well-written contract. This day and age contracts are available all over the internet. What's important for you to know is to use the contracts which have the specific clauses required for your project which provide you with the deliverables you need and have rock-solid verbiage to ensure there is no ambiguity or flexibility for the contractors to provide you with inadequate service. Contracts have several basic components:

- They will contain the license numbers or qualifications of contractors.

- The names of the company owners and contact information such as address and phone.
- The complete scope of work for the construction project.
- Project start and end dates.
- Project cost which include labor and materials as well as the payment schedule.
- A list of the materials to be used in the project.
- A list of any required permits.
- The process for change orders to the contract.
- And ultimately, the signature of the contractor and the client.

These are some common mistakes that construction company owners make. Not being sure that your quality standards for your contract includes the wording to obtain what you actually mean. By this I mean, if you say "contractor grade carpet" in the bathroom and "contractor grade paint" on the bathroom walls. This may mean an entirely different thing to the contractor you use. You may assume that this may be a "medium grade" low-cost material, whereas your contractor may purchase the cheapest paint possible in an 18 liter/5 gallon bucket and water it down with two more additional gallons of water as they spray. Meanwhile, you assume you will have a certain weight to your carpet and find that the carpet is so thin it's almost unusable for a client who purchases your final product such as a remodel or refurbishment.

14. Not using a contract. This is a common mistake that people run into. It occurs when they find someone that looks good on sight and agree to start work based on intuition. This will almost always come back to bite you when there is an oral agreement to work but the agreement is not backed up on paper. This will always result in payment disagreements and work completion disagreements.

15. Not checking for a license is another common problem, which has been discussed. Tradesman licenses are required for most home-improvement, remodel, repair, alteration, construction, or demolition projects whether residential or commercial. Tradesmen in the UK are required to hold a CSCS card as a level of health & safety competence. If the tradesman is working with Gas, they are required to be GasSafe Registered and if they are working with Electricity they are required to be registered with either, the NICEIC, Napit or ECA.

16. Failing to check references this is a common mistake. Always request references and review contractor's websites if possible for more information.

17. Always make sure you get more than one bid. Remember two principles. One is you often get what you pay for, and two, when you except just a single bid, you always think in the back of your mind you should've gotten other bids.

18. Make sure contractors are insured. If they are not insured make sure specific requirements are listed in your contract. Quite often if a contractor does not have insurance and is working on your project, you will ultimately be responsible for any injuries or accidents.

Administrative and Virtual employees:

During the economic downturn of 2007-2008 many professionals who were out of work began undertaking freelance opportunities. Companies during this time also needed to reduce costs and began outsourcing activities, which did not necessarily require a full or part time employee. The result was that businesses learned they could operate more efficiently by only hiring employees as needed and there was no need for paid benefits from the company. The benefit was twofold. Companies realized how to more effectively manage their resources and costs for labor in their activities. The second benefit was that freelancing was more prominent as an industry as companies learned of the flexibility of freelance employment. You hire the best freelancer based on their bid and portfolio. If the work is not adequate you sever ties but do not have the human resource headaches or interpersonal issues of having an employee in your face because you are letting them go.

CHAPTER 8

HOW TO PRICE FOR YOUR WORK AND SETTING YOUR PRICE

Are you a busy fool? This was something I fell into the trap of when I first started out. I was trying to price everything that came in and more. I now have a rule that I will only price a job for a client four times and if I do not get any feedback or acknowledgement I will not price anymore for that customer. You can be a busy fool, if you are pricing for a builder or construction company, they will be pricing for a job along with a minimum of another four contractors who in turn will have sent out information for pricing to their subcontractors the same as you. So let's say they have sent it out to four electrical contractors and there are four main contractors, then essentially there are sixteen electrical contractors pricing for the same job. Now your odds are stacked against you here and the job will tend to be won on price which isn't a position you want to be in as if you tend to win a job on price you have generally made a mistake when pricing it if you are the lowest.

The position you want to be in is where you get feedback from your customer to where your quote was compared with your competition. If you are always coming fourth on each project you are pricing for them, then you know you need to look at your pricing and you will need to make a commercial decision on whether to drop your price or not. If you keep pricing a customer and they give you no feedback, then I wouldn't bother pricing for them as you are just being used for a pricing exercise. It's not exactly ethical but you will find some contractors have preferred sub-contractors who they will pass your information onto so they can undercut you. I know this is wrong but it happens and you need to be aware of it.

If you are pricing in the domestic market, keep away from the people that want the cheapest price, don't waste your time. There will always be somebody cheaper than you. When they talk to you on the phone when enquiring for the job, you will get a feeling for what type of people they are. There are questions that you can ask subtly over the phone that will identify whether they want something for nothing or whether they want a service. Keep away from the people that want something for nothing. You will not build a successful business working for people like this. Let somebody else do it.

Quoting / Bidding/Tender

Pricing your services as a tradesman or construction company is the single most important business decision you can make. Setting prices too high or too low significantly limits your business growth. This will also result in issues with cash flow and sales. You should be very hands-on with your pricing strategy and increasing your profitability. You also have to be aware of your services compared to your competition. This is called building your pricing strategy. Your pricing strategy ensures that your cost and pricing are combined so that your business is profitable.

There are many pricing strategies that you can use within your company. Some of the basics are discussed here but further discussion can be found at Tradesman-Academy.com including in-depth analysis and financial modeling. It's important to first understand your basic cost and value principles. The cost of your service is the pound or dollar value that you spend to actually produce a final product or project. The price you set is your financial gain or reward in return for providing the final product or service. Value is what your customer feels that your project or product or service is worth to them.

An example of value is say for instance you are an electrical contractor. Wiring to a kitchen has failed. It may cost you £11.77 ($20 USD) in travel, £11.77 ($20 USD) in parts, and an hour of labor for which you charge £26.48 ($45 USD) in total you have £50.03 ($85 USD) invested in this repair however the homeowner who needs to cook dinner for their family places of value on this repair in a much higher rate so ultimately the electrician may charge £88.28 ($150 USD) for the repair. £88.28 ($150 USD) is the value of your work.

In order for you to best price your services or final projects you must have a feel for the perceived benefits the customer gains from buying your services. Understand what criteria they use in their decisions for a purchase of the service or project. Whether that be timeliness, quality, reliability, or convenience. Your value is the perceived recognition of value customers place on receiving the services you provide. So you should be setting your prices which reflect your value not just your cost.

In order for you to properly price your work it is important to understand fixed cost and variable cost. Every business is out to make a profit. Accurately reflecting your cost is critical in the pricing of your services or final product. The **fixed cost** is a cost that is always present, it doesn't matter how much work you sell. These include things such as salaries, rent, business fees, or equipment cost.

Variable costs increase as your company sales increase. These are additional costs such as additional material costs, additional labor costs, or additional use of your vehicle fleet because you have an increased volume of business.

Let's say you have a plumbing company and you charge £1,883.50 ($3,200 USD) for plumbing a retail store. And you have fixed cost of £23,543.76 ($40,000 USD) a year. In doing the math at £1,883.50 ($3,200 USD) per job you must sell or complete at least 13 jobs just to cover the overhead for that calendar year.

Cost plus pricing is when you take your cost of producing a service and adding the amount you need to make for a profit. This is most often a percentage of the cost. **Value-based pricing** is a scenario where you price based on what you believe the customers are willing to pay for your project or service. Value-based pricing depends on your strength as a business owner to sell your quality and benefits to a customer using your company.

As a business owner you have to decide what you want to use, cost-plus or value-based pricing. Cost-plus is a common method. Value-based pricing is a little less quantitative and relies more on qualitative pricing. To begin, you need to determine what your competitors are offering in terms of services and what they charge for them. You will want to set your price within range but not significantly higher or lower without good reason. If you price too high you will lose customers. And, if you price too low you'll have less profit. Remember the customers are willing to pay based on the perception of your quality.

There are various pricing tactics you can use with your business. Initially you'll work on market penetration. This will involve starting or offering your services or project at a lower price until you gained significant market share and then are able to increase your prices up to match your competition. To do so you will need to work on maintaining a loyal customer base and raise prices at a later time.

You may want to use what is called a **loss leader tactic** where you sell your services at a lower price and somewhat at a loss and although you do not make profit on this initial project you attract customers who purchase your more profitable services such as electrical wiring or plumbing. Meaning you may sell a drywall job at a lesser price in order to receive the plumbing and electrical components which you may charge more reasonable prices. This is a tag and or lead-in for future business. You may also want to use what is called the **discounting method**. In the discounting method you reduce prices in order to encourage larger orders. This would be a bidding situation where you bid say the wiring of 30 domestic or residential homes. You offer a discount for doing this large number of homes but also make more profit as you are working with a higher volume of work. Remember if you are purchasing more material quantities you should also be receiving larger discounts from your suppliers too.

The next tactic is called **value pricing.** This is used in your bids where you make your pricing appear more attractive. An example of this is say painting a bedroom.

Let's say you're going to place a quote at £410 in order to perform the painting. On your quote sheet you should indicate £395. £$395 is very close to £$410 yet on paper and to the purchaser it looks significantly lower.

or

Let's say you're going to place a quote at $700 in order to perform painting & decorating a bedroom. On your quote sheet you should indicate $685. $685 is very close to $700 yet on paper and to the purchaser it looks significantly lower.

You also need to be keen on when to raise or lower prices. There are times when this needs to fluctuate based on the economy and you should always be performing an analysis during your 90 minutes (discussed in chapter 10) to determine impact on your profitability if you change prices. When increasing prices you will improve your profitability even though your total sales volume drops. When reducing prices, you may do so to take on additional work. But remember, lowering prices may also indicate to potential clients that your quality of service is less.

Each business owner should be familiar with the basics of bidding and develop strategies which work for them based on whether their businesses electrical, plumbing, mechanical, structural, or architectural in nature. Each type of trade varies and you will rely on your experience to place the best bids. Having said that, it is important to understand some of the basic components for bidding, proposing, or tendering.

Remember this, when low bidders win jobs, the low bid most often results in delays and unnecessary change orders. When these same bidders bid low to "get their foot in the door" and the project does not go as planned they usually go out of business within a year or two because they cannot sustain this type of financial loss.

When you are bidding, be aware of the potential costs you may have to absorb and determine at what point you do not absorb the costs. By this I mean there are customers you would never hand over a small change order for something a sub contractor forgot. You lose too much good will with them for future jobs and appear as if you are trying to squeeze every penny out of the customer.

Let's discuss bid package components:

- The **bid package** or tender document consist of the drawings and a project manual or specification which contains information on the structural, mechanical, electrical, and plumbing scope of works.
- **Construction bids** are an actual offer to perform work for a specified price.
- **Price** is the amount of compensation for your labor, materials, equipment usage, and profit.

- The **project manual** or **Tender Document** is a book which has an invitation for you to place a bid, the bid requirements, instructions for placing the bid, experience requirement forms.
- The actual **contract**.
- **Regulations, rules, and laws** related to labor, inspections, licenses, regulations, permits, and taxes.
- **Special conditions** such as environmental applications.
- **Waste disposal, storage, and utilities.**
- **Technical specifications** for tradesmen including drawings and   specifications

"**A good bid** is one which is submitted by a reliable contractor with no omissions, accurate time reflections, accurate price-out for subcomponents, plans for any difficulties which arise, fair market markup for profit, an explanation of insurance and an alternate approach to bids."

Let's look at some of the key components to help you with a good bidding strategy. Experienced bidders incorporate long-range planning with attention to detail into their bids. This is incorporated early in their bidding process.

Let's start with the site walk through. After you've looked at the bid documents and have a general idea of the project you want to arrange a visit to the construction job site. You may already have some ideas on quantities and material requirements before you visit the job site.

Once you have the bid documents available you may do a preliminary take off on materials required for the job. Take your original take off to the job site and make detailed notes which you may want to submit to the owner of the project before you submit your bid. By performing the job site walk to you are able to investigate the site and the conditions to determine whether your bid is going to make money for you or not. Make notes of the differences between what are in the contract documents and what you actually see on the job site so you can get clarification from the project owner or the main contractor. Keep in mind all of these issues when you place your bid: Site security, the ease of getting to and from the job site, additional safety requirements or storage requirements and the soil conditions. What sources of electricity and water are available at the job site? How far would your subcontractors be traveling? You may want to take photographs of some of the site conditions you are unsure of to review when you get back to the office.

Okay let's run you through some of the basic fundamentals of submitting a successful bid package. Remember you can always access more detailed bidding strategies at Tradesman-Academy.com.

The project manual or tender document is the same thing as a specifications book. It contains the scope of work, conditions, wage rates, special conditions, payment terms, questions, estimates, take off sheets, the bid package, and pricing. Here are some sample checklists you may want to take with you.

The first is a sample estimating worksheet.

Estimating worksheet			Page number		
Job Title	Master Bathroom Ellingsworth Apartment				
Date	March 21, 2014				
Job description – Installation of a new tub, faucet, and toilet for an apartment at loft 12.					
Description	Quantity	Materials	Unit Price	Labor	Total
Tub installation	1	Tub			$355.79
	2	PVC 1 ½"	$2.30		
	2	PVC 2"	$2.62		
	3	Elbows male	0.38		
	3	Elbows female	0.33		
	1	Cleaner	$3.24		
	1	Tub	$346.92		

The second is a site visit checklist.

Project Name	Anderson Township Flats
Location Address	Mr. David Smith 16 Whetstone Street LONDON EC1Y 9SY UNITED KINGDOM
Travel distance to jobsite	4 km
Site conditions:	Unlevel for material storage. Rocky terrain with minimal space between adjoining property fence.
Roadways	Reliable access to major streets
Soil data and reports	Site location is wet and roadbed is dirt in composition. Large trucks will not support delivery of materials.
	Most materials will require lift delivery to the third floor
Height to work	
	One chain gate for entry
Gates	
Security	No onsite security...bring padlocks
Available electricity	Electrical 60A and 100A service on site
Available water	Yes
Telephone	No must use personal cell
Waste disposal	Not provided will require order
Parking	Minimal only 3 spaces for workers

Comment section: John Whitmire is my point of contact. It is expected to rain Monday, Tuesday and Wednesday. First available material delivery is Thursday.

The third is a sample construction bid.

Tradesman Drywall Company			
Job Description: Drywall and paint ceilings. Sharpe retail stores:			
Phone	Date	Email	
Estimated start	Estimated finish		
Square footage for 1/2 ceilings	Sq ft	Unit price	Total
Square footage for 5/8 ceilings	Sq ft	Unit price	Total
Square footage for 1/2 wallboard	Sq ft	Unit price	Total
Square footage for 5/8 wallboard	Sq ft	Unit price	
Texture installation spray			
		Total	

Each trade has its own set of tips and tricks to successfully bid a job. For example, on an **electrical job,** always start by reading the specifications to determine your scope of work. Pay keen attention to the general conditions. Answer these questions:

Is any special insurance required?

Is this project tax exempt?

How much of my pay or draws are held prior to release?

Who furnishes/provides temporary power?

Who pays for the temporary power?

Are there any allowances?

Are there any alternates?

What progress reports are required?

Are security deposits or bonds required?

What is the process for damages?

Are there any labor intensive items?

Are there floors or areas that are the same so you can gain efficiency?

Being aware of the "what-ifs" will go a long way to keep you from getting stuck with charges you hadn't anticipated.

Example: Some key things to be aware of when bidding plumbing jobs that the other guys typically forget or leave out of their bids are:

- Minimise your acceptance of risk during core drilling to say a maximum size of 50mm.
- Make sure your bid states you do not remove or replace deteriorated pipe you discover during your work.
- If there is an added cost for a performance bond for a job make sure you include it.
- Your bid does not cover costs related to temporary installations such as faucets or temporary toilets.
- You do not provide white goods such as washing machines unless they are included in your bid.
- Who is responsible for offsite soil and dirt removal or disposal?
- Only provide the backflow valves required on the plumbing drawings.
- Your responsibility for ceiling or wall repair or removal should only be done if it is listed in the scope of work. This responsibility would normally reside with the general contractor.
- **Don't forget** permits, bonds, or fees. You'll be responsible for them if you don't exclude them in your bid.
- Make it clear in your bid that you do not repair code violations or none conforming regulation work uncovered during your remodel work that are not part of the original bid.
- And last, make sure your bid states that you do not shut down, drain down and perform the subsequent refilling of domestic water piping when performing a remodel or

refurbishment. Pipefitters may be required to do this for fire regulations/code, but your average plumber does not want to be responsible for draining and filling a large building.

Here are some quick tips for **drywall trade** bidding:

- Keep up on your geometry, visualize rectangular sheets on the wall and use a smartphone app or use grid paper to draw diagrams to scale for each separate area of the building's interior. Once the diagrams are drawn, then sketch out the most efficient panel configuration.
- Encourage the building owner to use mold resistant drywall in applications which are high in moisture content and include it in your bid.
- Make sure you know the current code requirements in your area and the regulations/code requirements for new products. Different thicknesses are required for different applications and the regulations/code can vary significantly for fire applications depending on the region. Also, although a supplier may sell new drywall applications and materials, they may not meet the code requirements for your specific job.

Summary of Chapter 8 - Remember the key to winning a bid is to use quality work not low pricing. You have to remember to position your trade or construction business in the right strategic stance you have to sell your quality and consistency. Think in these terms: 1) Your work is always the best quality and you have expertise that others do not have. 2) Your projects are always on time and without delay. 3) Your projects are clear in their representation and will be on budget 4) You are a contractor with great integrity. Your reputation is what you sell.

Your bid package should contain necessary information on the structural, mechanical, electrical, and plumbing plans as well as carpentry to be done on a project with your actual offer to perform work and specified price.

Remember a good bid is one which is submitted by a reliable contractor with no omissions, accurate time reflections, accurate price-out for subcomponents, plans for any difficulties which arise, fair market markup for profit, an explanation of insurance and an alternate approach to bids.

In order for you to properly price your work it is important to understand fixed cost and variable cost. Every business is out to make a profit. Accurately reflecting your cost is critical in the pricing of your services or final product.

Quoting and bidding your services as a tradesman or construction company is the single most important business decision you can make. Setting prices too high or too low significantly limits your business growth.

CHAPTER 9

BEING CAREFUL OF THE BIGGER BOYS

As you grow your business you will inevitably be approaching larger businesses to price work for or place bids for projects and contracts if you are in the commercial and industrial market sectors. Working for these types of companies can be good to elevate your business into growing, as you want it too. Now for one minute I am not saying that every large business out there is out to screw you, but there are a few that will try to. So I just want to make you aware of this so that you can go down that damage limitation route again. There are a few things I would advise doing before working for the "bigger boys" as I call them.

The first thing I would do if I were for example a plumbing company is develop a targeted list of business or construction companies within 100 miles of my business. I would initially go to a freelance website such as elance.com or peopleperhour.com and put a job advert for a researcher to find say 200 building / construction companies with over 10 employees within a 100 miles radius of your business. You will probably pay between £29 - £117 or $50 - $200 dollars for this service. Once you have the list

I would then check them out financially using a web service to find out their profits for last year, their turnover, if they are good payers etc. Once I have sorted out the better more viable companies I would then target say 20 of them initially by calling them or sending them your information by direct mail to get on their supplier list.

Once they ask you to start pricing work, inquire about payment terms. If their terms are more than 30 days or 45 days at a push, I probably wouldn't price the work for them.

If you do decide to price work for the company, make sure you provide a quotation that details information. A sample can be found on the Tradesman Academy website. At a minimum make sure you clarify exactly what you are doing and more importantly what you are not doing. What is in the project requirements and what is out of the project requirements?

Also, detail what you expect the contractor to be doing for you at no cost. If the company has a QS (Quantity Surveyor) working for them, it is their job to do what I call "subbie bashing" which is where they will do whatever they can to reduce your payments and make more profit for them. An example of this that I come across a lot is the use of skips. What a main contractor will do is say that you have used their skips on site to remove your rubbish as well as their labour for cleaning the rubbish up. Let's say they deduct $200 of each company on site to remove rubbish and there are 10 companies on site which they do the same to. Essentially they have made an extra $2000.00 dollars on the job, which they will get away with if they can. Be careful.

Credit limits, I will generally give any new companies a credit limit which I will work up to until I have established a trustworthy relationship with them. So for example I would give a new company that I do work for a limit of £10,000, ($16,000 USD) which would need to be cleared before I carry out any further work for them. This should limit your risk when working with new customers.

One thing you need to do when competing with the bigger boys is to determine your market size. What are the monetary value of projects you want to work on? So for example, you allow the company to work up to a project value of £ 58,859.40 ($100,000 USD) to keep your cash flow healthy. This is one thing you need to determine when you develop your niche in the market and decide what you can bid on. This includes what you can responsibly manage with your span of control using the contractors you have. You may also want a mix of residential, retail, or commercial type projects. This is all a matter of personal preference.

Depending on the economic conditions, small tradesman or construction companies may find themselves competing with larger companies on almost constant basis. This takes a little bit of strategic thought as a business owner to determine your niche market. Quite often smaller companies are able to find a niche in government projects because they qualify for small, disabled, or minority type of jobs. Having a small company is an advantage because the government often provides work to a smaller company in order to provide economic stimulus. In this case you have the upper hand.

Many government entities also have a required minimum number of contracts which must be awarded to small businesses. This provides you the upper hand as well. In addition, the approval process or paperwork required to place a bid for these jobs has been significantly streamlined over the last few years. This requires you to spend less time with the paperwork and more time on bidding where the law of averages may work in your favor. Your key to outmaneuvering and outperforming the bigger guys is to focus on your website presence and aggressively marketing your portfolio. Great tips for your marketing programs can be found at Tradesman-Academy.com.

Another key advantage that you have as a smaller guy is that you have the flexibility with contracted staff. You have less overhead costs and more agility than the larger boys. Quite often they bid low on projects so they can just make payroll.

Summary of Chapter 9 - As you grow your business you will inevitably be approaching larger businesses to price work for or place bids for projects and contracts if you are in the commercial and industrial market sectors. There are a few things I would advise doing before working for the "bigger boys" as I call them. The first thing I would do is develop a targeted list of business or construction companies within 100 miles of my business. Sort out the better more viable companies' say 20 of them initially by calling them or sending them your information by direct mail to get on their supplier list. Provide a quotation that details information and watch out for "subbie bashing" which is where they will do whatever they can to reduce your payments and make more profit for them.

CHAPTER 10

WORKING ON YOUR BUSINESS INSTEAD OF IN IT. TAKE TIME OUT - YOUR 90 MINUTES - DON'T WASTE YOUR TIME IN THE DAY

The one thing that you need to get right in your business is the time that you spend on your business and not in it. This is the difference between the successful business owners out there and the mediocre ones. You see, spending time on your business instead of in it is the most important thing that you need to do if you want to achieve success. The reason for this is that the most important thing for your business and you to succeed is to get and keep customers and your client base. Ask yourself the question, when are you getting customers today, then where does it fit into your schedule? There is a mentor of mine that has taught me that if you don't spend time getting new and keeping your existing customers, you will soon be without them, therefore it is imperative that you spend an allocated time of your working day focusing on getting and keeping customers.

I try and keep to this schedule as best as I can and I spend around 90 minutes a day working to grow my business as it is a key part of the business success. The people I know that employ this technique have had more success in their business than those who don't. It doesn't really matter when you do it in the day but do it in one chunk and make sure you are not disturbed. You may be a morning person and do it first thing. I tend to start my 90 minutes at 4 O'clock every day as this tends to be the quietest time for me and allows me to get things done. The majority of my success in business has been derived from my 90 minute chunks and that's how important these 90 minutes are. Get yourself into the zone and really implement stuff in the 90 minutes, you will be surprised at what you can achieve. Don't spend your time doing menial tasks that somebody else can do. Get a part time assistant if need be. If you think you cannot afford to do it, then you really should be thinking you cannot afford to not have one. Your aim over time is to generate more money coming in by getting new business than it costs you to employ an assistant for 5 hours per week.

Once you get into a pattern, you will find that over months, you will get busier with more customers and it will become natural. The only problem here is that you use your time effectively for business growth purposes. It's no good using your allotted time a day of say 60 minutes to answer e-mails or order your online shopping for the weekend, you need to be focused to enable you to get the most out of the time. Make sure you segregate yourself from others, whether in an office or at home, make sure you cannot be disturbed, and make sure everybody around you knows this.

A key thing to remember when outsourcing to others is that around 80% of what you do can be done by others. Don't get hung up on somebody else not doing it as good as you. You may be right, but as long as they do a competent job of it, then that is sufficient enough for your business and allows you the time needed to grow your business.

Tips for your allotted time:
- Turn your phone off, you can always divert it to somebody else.
- Don't open your e-mails as you become somebody else's agenda then.
- Don't open post.
- Get yourself into an environment where you will not be distracted by background noise.
- If you have staff, make sure they know you are not to be disturbed.

You are allowed a cup of tea!

What you do in your 90 minutes?

Have a plan and develop a routine. You need a clear goal, if you have decided that you need to bring in $90,000 a month then this is a clear goal and you need to work towards this.

It's important to give yourself deadlines in your marketing. So for example, you are allowing yourself 60 minutes a day to get customers and keep them. So you may allocate 20 minutes to going through your AdWords account and making changes. You may give yourself 40 minutes to write a direct sales letter, the following day, you may give yourself 60 minutes to research a type of customer in a geographical area that you are going to send the direct mail out that you did yesterday. Make sure you get the stuff done and don't procrastinate. The following day, give yourself 30 minutes to write a follow up direct mail letter and then 30 minutes to write an e-mail that will be sent to your existing clients. Get my drift. To give you an idea of some of the things I do:

1. E-mail - Draft e-mails to be sent out to your e-mail list (Not replying to emails but business growth emails)
2. Direct mail
3. Auto responder campaigns
4. Google AdWords
5. Follow up letters
6. Squeeze pages
7. Drafting offers of the month
8. Sifting my database

9. Creating copy for adverts

10. Facebook

11. Twitter

12. Reviewing my websites

You should always be in the mindset to be working on your business not just in it. Always thinking in a mindset of "what would I have others do if I could afford to have them do it? In the business world this is called "opportunity cost". Meaning, what could you be doing of more importance if you were not dealing with something of little importance. There are some other tips that you can use during your 90 minutes a day. Tips on working on your business and not in it. These tips help you develop a strategic standpoint, which helps, separate your average business owner from those who truly excel and build great businesses. A handful are shown here but even more strategic points are shown in Tradesman-Academy.com.

- Spend some time one day refining your niche market. This helps to differentiate your product from your competitors. Instead of focusing on routinely firing off bids to jobs in the hope to win a deal. Take time to develop marketing, which explains why your work is undeniably better than that of your competition.

- Take time to invest in your community. What do you have to offer your community as far as time, resources or volunteerism? This in turn will work out well for marketing communication and community relations and also goodwill in your community. This works twofold. One, it's the right thing to do for your community. Two, you have the opportunity to be shown on websites, newspapers, and other media as a community leader who not only excels at quality in your trade but also in giving back to the community.

- Always remember to thank your existing clients if it's nothing more than a thank you card, a pen, or a notepad. Always remember this is marketing for your organization and helps build client relationships. Take that extra time out in your 90 minutes a day to thank those who have given you business and encourage them to provide you more business in the future.

- Have another person review your website with you. Have them walk you through the pages and explain it from their perspective. Have them look at your portfolio and rate it on a scale of 1 to 10 to you. Ask how likely they would be to use you as the provider for their project.

- Having someone else review your webpage will give you an additional set of eyes to notice issues that you may not see yourself because you see it so frequently or because you have a closeness to your projects.

- Take some time in your 90 minutes to identify a task that is time-consuming which you could outsource. Make a list of the small tasks that you do including research, filing, or other tasks which you could free up some additional time so you can focus strategically on your work and the growth of your business.

- Take some time out to learn about one aspect that you least know about your business. Learn something such as the conversion rate for your webpage. Set a goal to increase your conversion rate by 1% this would be a significant boost in revenue for your business.
- Focus some of your 90 minutes per day to increase your companies visibility on social media sites this includes Facebook, twitter, etc.

Spend your time working on your business not in your business. Your major function should be the growth of your company and creating wealth to grow your business. It's your responsibility to strategically monitor and know when to add an additional van, purchase specialized tools, or an additional team member to your business. This growth will occur through your marketing, network, and planning. This will be totally dependent on you finding the time to network and market your business and plan for expansion. Make sure you are setting milestones for the next level of business growth for your company. As the business owner you should have your strategic vision on paper. Know your capabilities and your core competencies and realize your true potential through sustainable competitive advantage.

What do you need to do differently every day in your operations to meet your full potential? What do you need to offer your clients and customers? What portion of your business do you need to look at possibly stopping or abandoning in the future to take on work which complements your portfolio or is more aligned with your business functions? What other workers do you need to bring on board to your company to make it more successful? What are the financial resources you need? What are the competencies you need? What specialized tools could you use or equipment to help you achieve your goals and objectives? Do you have the right people, in the right place, with the right resources, at the right time? What is your plan to invest in this to achieve your big objective? And, what are your competitors doing in response to what you are doing? This is your competitive strategy. Need more ideas for this? Visit Tradesman-Academy.com.

Summary of Chapter 10 – Your 90 minute chunks are one of the key drivers for your long-term success. I try and keep to this schedule as best as I can and I spend around 90 minutes a day working to grow my business as it is a key part of the business success. The majority of people I know employ this technique and it has been successful for them. The majority of my success in business has been derived from my 90 minute chunks. Use this time for key business growth such as drafting e-mail to be sent out to e-mail lists, develop direct mail, auto responder campaigns, Google Adwords, send follow up letters, develop squeeze pages, draft offers of the month, sift databases, create copy for adverts and focus on search engine optimization and social media links.

CHAPTER 11

STRATEGIC GROWTH FOR EXISTING CONSTRUCTION COMPANIES

Management of a trade or construction business can be a challenging endeavor. Economic market changes, material costs, and labor markets fluctuate. Managing your company should become easier over time as you develop sustainable processes which deliver consistent projects. How you weather the market changes in comparison to your competition and depends on your strategy and savvy as a business owner.

A trade or construction business strategy is founded on your vision, use of innovation, growth, and marketing. What tools do you need to develop consistent quality for an increasingly larger portfolio or projects? What do you need to meet the new challenges for your business? Here's a roadmap I have developed over time.

Think in a strategic mindset

What type of strategic plan have you developed and how are you tracking your progress towards it in your 90 minutes a day? What are your biggest obstacles? Write them down. Develop your goals in the context of the current state or "reality" for your business. What opportunities do you have and what are your steps towards meeting these opportunities?

Use the SWOT method for analysis of your business

Make a quick chart to help you visualize your company's Strengths, Weaknesses Opportunities, and Threats (SWOT). What capabilities do you have in terms of your resources and experience? What issues do you see for business related to economic and market trends? Give yourself a visual and work from it.

Typical SWOT analysis consist of Leadership & Corporate Culture, Organization Structure & Behavior, Employees, Operations & Processes, Product/ Service, Pricing, Materials, Logistics, Distribution, Supply Chain, Market Research, Information Technology, Financial, Industry Structure, Specific Competition,

Population and Demographics, and Legal, Regulatory, and Political aspects.

Here's a sample:

Shrewsbury Electrical Company
SWOT Analysis

Strengths

- Your abilities and experience
- Resources such as tools and equipment
- Established network of subcontractors
- Marketing and SEO experience
- Construction apps
- Geographical location to jobsites
- Price, value and quality
- You use 90 minute chunks and the competition does not

Weaknesses

- Missing skills
- Cash flow
- Continuity
- Lack of planning
- Reliability or outsourced employees
- Lack of a strategic plan

Opportunities

- New equipment
- New products
- New area developments
- Innovation and technology
- Alliances with other trades needing your work
- Niche markets

Threats

- Political and economic effects
- New code laws
- Competitive intentions
- Market demand
- New environmental laws management strategies

Focus on your marketing plan

What are your competitors doing for marketing? Have you received a sales communication in the mail and thought "I wish my advertising looked this good". Market your new services. What are the current trends? Are your neighbors having concrete edging or stamped concrete installed?

Focus on past customers for additional business

Determine what percentage of repeat business you would like to have in comparison to new customers. What ratio do you have 80 percent new / 20 percent existing client base?

Evaluate your market share

What percentage of the local market do you actually own? .001%, 1%, 5%? How do you know? How many electrical contractors are in your area? How many plumbers?

Spend some time on your budget

Do an analysis of your cost over the last year. Make sure it is in alignment with prior year spending. What had increased most, cable costs, plumbing fixtures, equipment rentals, fuel costs, roofing slates? Find new suppliers. Above all, ask for discounts and better rates and payment terms I.E. 60 days

Networking and knowledge

How are you networking with others in your industry? Do you attend trade conferences? Remember from earlier discussion, what trades can you team up with yours? Every plumber needs a drywall guy. Every drywall guy needs a painter. How are you building your knowledge? Continuing Education Units, trades courses, local code / regulations training? Many avenues exist from online suppliers for free training on energy efficiency and how to install products. Take time out to make yourself better.

Improve productivity and efficiency

How can you work smarter? Use technology and collaboration. Many businesses are employing "Lean" principles. In lean six sigma you methodically analyze your processes to remove "non-value added" steps in each process. Leaning processes can result in 20 to 50 percent savings. For more information on optimizing your business using Lean visit Tradesman-Academy.com

Technology leveraging

What new technology is available for your business? Hundreds of new Technology apps are developed each week for every field, concrete, masonry, roofing, framing, electrical and HVAC. These are real time savers for project management, budget tracking, bid placement, scheduling, photos and tracking.

Maintain a consistent pipeline of new opportunities

Would it be bad to have too much work? Maybe, but probably not. How do you get yourself in that type of situation? Through good marketing and research. Try pursuing government contracts.

Warranty work

Warranty work or refurbishments / remodels may be a niche market for you if you can establish larger contracts with companies or possible multi-facility bids.

Tips for optimizing your trade or construction business for growth:

Construction is one of the largest sectors of the United Kingdom economy. It contributes almost £90 billion to the UK economy (or 6.7%) in value added, comprises over 280,000 businesses covering some 2.93 million jobs, which is equivalent to about 10% of total UK employment. (*Source, ONS Annual Business Survey). The construction and trades industry has suffered disproportionately since the recession of 2008 but is growing and this is the time to focus your strategy which economists say is key for you to take advantage of green and sustainable construction opportunities. The economy growth will be dependent on having the right tradesmen with the needed skills. You want to be the most skilled person in your trade or at least have the most quality. Innovation is going to be the second most important factor. This includes how well you collaborate with the other trades on your jobsite to complete a project, marketing innovation such as SEO, and how much new knowledge you gain as a tradesman.

The trades sector has always been a historically significant sector providing fuel for growth in economic downturns. For you that equals opportunity.

In order for you to meet the challenges of business growth and the competition of your competitors you have to apply the right level of intensity to your operations both daily and long term. One idea that can really help you out in this area is standardization.

Standardization of daily operating practices is a key component of today's Lean construction management practices. Remember from earlier that Lean is used to remove processes that add cost to your doing business but don't add value.

Standardization - What standardization helps you to do is increase your accuracy, productivity, and efficiency. When you arrive on the jobsite would you prefer to show up with a truck that has ladders, extension cords, supplies, compressors all in a pile or neatly arranged so you know where your tools are, parts are, and materials are? This is just an example of how standardization and organization help your efficiency. In lean this is called the 5S method which stands for Sort, Straighten, Shine, Standardize, and Sustain.

Increased accuracy, productivity, and efficiency lead to greater quality and increased profits for you. You should be using standardization in every project. Being able to consistently reproduce products with the same result in quality but with less cost or time should be your goal.

Documentation - always document your projects including issues with the project and customer service problems. Good documentation helps in proving work was done, helps with disagreements in cost, and helps with better cash flow management.

Rework / Snagging - Focus on your plan to reduce rework and punch / snag lists. This should go without saying, but the idea to take away here is make sure you improve with every project.

Estimates - Work to improve the accuracy of your estimates. Better estimates most often result in winning job bids and winning job bids keeps a constant flow of work to your business.

Lean process thinking - Try this for your trade or construction projects. For projects that are routine. Use one of your 90 minute chunks to write down the steps in a project from your initial bid until you receive final payment. How many steps are there? 40?, 85?, 200? Since these jobs are repetitive try to eliminate steps that add no value or add nothing to the job. This is your reduction in cycle time. Over time you can reduce the work and effort for a project 20 to 40 percent. Lean improves project flow and eliminates bottlenecks.

Sustainable projects - Sustainable trade work and construction projects are in demand today. Sustainable projects reduce waste and pollution. They minimize energy use during construction. Sustainable projects protect the environment. Being a sustainable builder may give you an advantage with some clients or major contracts. There are many green construction opportunities in the UK market. The global green and sustainable building industry is forecast to grow at an annual rate of 22.8% between now and 2017 (*source IBIS World) which are a result of increasing low carbon regulatory requirements and greater societal demand for greener products. This means additional opportunity for you.

Good execution - Most failures of trades or construction companies are caused by poor operational execution. Each year in the UK and in the US 50% of new companies go out of business. Within 3 years that number approached 80%. Look around at your competition. Many of them are only a project or two away from complete failure and bankruptcy. Your success depends on day to day business management and an infusion of best practices. Your personal goal should be to fall within the top 25% of the other tradesman and contractors in your area...not the middle...and not in the bottom 25%.

Summary of Chapter 11 - Strategic growth for existing construction and tradesman companies determines future growth. Management of a trade or construction business can be a challenging endeavor because of economic markets, material costs, and labor market fluctuation. Your strategy should involve daily business operations combined with good project management functioning in tandem with strategy execution, marketing for growth, and consistent use of your 90 minute chunks.

Always look at your business with a strategic mindset. Use the SWOT method for analysis of your business to determine your strengths, weaknesses, opportunities, and threats. Always look for new ways to improve productivity and efficiency. Your 90 minute chunks should be doing this for you. Remember to evaluate your market share, spend some time on your budget, network with other tradesman, and continually build your knowledge.

There are many tips for optimizing your trade or construction business for growth. With construction being one of the largest sectors of the United Kingdom economy there is plenty of opportunity for your business.

Standardization of daily operating practices is a key component of today's Lean construction management practices. Increased accuracy, productivity, and efficiency lead to greater quality and increased profits for you. You should be using standardization in every project. Minimize rework and if it occurs evaluate it. You should also improve your documentation and estimate accuracy. Remember most businesses fail because of bad execution. Don't let this be you. Your personal goal should be to fall within the top 25% of the other tradesman and contractors in your area...not the middle...and not in the bottom 25%.

CHAPTER 12

ADVANCED TACTICAL STRATEGIES – FINDING YOUR FOCUS

This chapter is designed to help you better formulate your business strategy. In the strategic growth chapter you saw how strategy tools can help improve your business. Now let's look at taking it up a notch with even more ideas and tools.

Use your 90 minute chunks per day to improve operational performance but also to build your strategy. What are you looking at, and what are you not looking at? What are your competitors looking at and what are the business professionals in your area looking at? What have you learned through networking? Is your company keeping up with technology? What performance metrics are you using? What are the cutting edge trends for your trade? What is important to you for success?

These are your key drivers:

- Internet marketing
- More services
- Better services

- Better portfolio
- Better customer service
- Decreased cost
- More efficiency
- Environmental and sustainability
- Community
- Lean initiatives (Non Value added activities)

You want your company to be this:

"Newcastle Plumbing Services" - Known for the highest quality service, friendly workers, reliability, trustworthy, uses water saving green products and supports local football teams.

The Tradesman-Academy can get you there.

The Tradesman-Academy can help you with tips and tools that will take your operations to the next level. Your decision to read From Tradesman to Business Man - How tradesman make their first million in 90 minute chunks indicates your desire to take your business to the next level.

Here is the formula for success:

Your Trade + Business savvy + 90 Minute Chunks = Your 1st Million

Look at your tradesman business from the outside in. How does the customer view your business? We have already discussed your image with business cards, vehicles and uniform appearance. Typically the customer has three main concerns with domestic trades projects and you should be prepared to address them. Their number one concern is the quality of the project or end result, the number two concern is the length of time the project will take, and the third most common concern is what mess will remain after the project. Don't let the poor workmanship of others reflect on your business.

What kinds of problems and concerns do you have? Material costs? Employing outsourced employees? Liability insurance?

Studies of small construction company owners show their biggest concerns are uncertainty of economic conditions, business taxation, employees, and technology. Here's the breakdown of the major groups of concerns.

1. Taxes

2. Regulations

3. Costs

4. Finance

5. Employees

6. Information

7. Management

8. Competition

9. Technology

So where do these fall as your concerns for your trade business? What are you doing with your 90 minute chunks to alleviate the concern for these? As a smart tradesman you don't want to let these concerns be your concerns. Make a list of your top concerns and develop a plan to address them through 90 minute chunks. When you network with other tradesmen and they say "I have this concern". You should be able to respond with "I had that concern also but here's the plan I developed to address it so it is not a concern for my company." Minimize your stress in these areas and you are well on your way to developing a strategic place in the market you work in.

Common Stressors for Tradesmen		
Taxes on business income	Government paperwork	Safety and health concerns
Cost of supplies and materials	High fixed costs	Marketing
Low profits	Qualified employees	Cash flow
Cost of professional services i.e. attorneys / solicitors	Control of my time	Keeping up on market developments
Licenses and permits	Delinquent accounts	Crime and vandalism to project
Business growth	Vehicles	Social media

Construction and trades business management are more difficult and require different strategies than any other business because of the nature of our work. So many of your activities are interdependent on others and require you to have good project management abilities. Let me give you some examples of conditions tradesmen encounter that other industries do not.

- You are required to make your new work fit in existing construction or with new code / regulation requirements.
- Trade work is often seasonal
- Every project is different
- Your process for each project may not be the same...but it should be
- Your cost may vary based on access to the jobsite or conditions of work you are remodeling / refurbishing
- You may have a difficult time in trying to automate any of your processes
- Managing utility usage can be difficult
- Difficult economic times leads to theft from your jobsite or from employees
- Your success depends on the outsourced or contracted people you use
- Your work has a greater impact caused by weather and the environment
- Delays in a job result in greater overhead costs for you and put you in a bind for cash flow
- Projects with extended durations impact and limit your ability to bid more jobs

You can always find more information on project management techniques at Tradesman-Academy.com

Trades and benchmarking

Increasing competition in your area, combined with market forces affecting higher material and labor costs, force the tradesman to improve the efficiency of their operations to be more competitive.

To maintain this strategy advanced tradesmen and construction business owners use **performance measurement**. Performance measurement tells you, the business owner, how you are doing and which direction your company is going. There are some business owners who always have a stable influx of jobs but never take it to the next level. They never really knew how they were doing just that they were above water and making some profit. If they better understood the measures they could impact them and take their business to the next level. Performance management for your company is based knowing what numbers to impact based on your situation. What numbers are you comparing to your competition? The way to know this is through benchmarking.

Benchmarking compares your measures to your competition in terms of your business management and financial stability. Benchmarking provides you valuable information related to your strategic vision and application of your "90 minute chunks per day".

Always benchmark with businesses that are the same size as yours, similar type work i.e. concrete, framing, electrical, and same sizes of projects i.e domestic or commercial.

Ok so what does benchmarking help me to do in my business?

Benchmarking uses measures from the "best performers in your trade" and helps you develop your plan for the next 1, 3, and 5 year periods based on marketing, growth opportunity seeking, restructuring, and financial management. Benchmarking helps you evaluate potential risk, your businesses strengths and weaknesses, and your potential comparative advantage in relation to other trades. You have to determine which processes are critical to your success.

Benchmarking is similar to your marketing development. Both of these should be reviewed frequently during your 90 minute chunks. Benchmarking is a continuous process of adjusting your operations to improve and become the best. Here are some of the activities you will do during your 90 minute chunks:

- Compare your activity with those within your region...who is the best and why?
- Compare what you offer for services and packages compared to your competition.
- Determine what technological applications would help you... new trade apps, new products, which have an easier and reduced installation time, faster drying, time, one

143

time application, or come in prefabricated pieces reducing your time requirements.

- Continually adjust to new trends to build your efficiency, quality and customer satisfaction.

There are three types of benchmarking you can do.

- Strategic benchmarking
- Process benchmarking
- Performance benchmarking

The benchmarking process includes deciding what you want to measure and how it will be performed. Deciding how and where you will collect data, measure your results, and determine your gaps. Your goal is to develop an action oriented plan aligned with your strategy.

Many studies have been performed including the Key Performance Indicators in the United Kingdom (KPI) and Construction Industry Institute Benchmarking and Metric (CII) which look at benchmarking.

Tradesman-Academy can help you look at the key performance indicators of productivity, client complaints, accident rates, deviation of project schedule, planning effectiveness, deviation of cost by project, efficiency of labour, subcontracting rates, and risk rates. Here are a few we can help you look at:

Performance Indicator	Measured component
Planning effectiveness	The percent % of planned projects and completed projects
Quality	Number of projects/number of customer complaints
Project scope	Initial sale / final sale
Project timeliness	Final due date/ initial due date/ the date you budgeted for
Cost	Final real cost – your cost/budgeted cost

Tradesman-Academy can help you with even more advanced measures such as total project duration, project growth cost, delta growth cost, phase duration factor, project schedule factor, delta budget factor, project budget factor, and more.

Here's a sample formula:

Project Cost Growth

$$\frac{\text{The Actual Total Project Cost – the Initial Predicted Project Cost}}{\text{Initial Predicted Project Cost}}$$

Key performance indicators (KPI) in the United Kingdom

The KPI Programme was initiated by the UK Best Practice Programme to enable measurement of project and organisational performance in the construction industry. Other studies have been performed through educational institutions such as the

Manchester Business School, University of Manchester, United Kingdom.

The construction and trade measures for the UK are framed under the groupings of Time, Cost, Quality, Client Satisfaction, Client Changes, Business Performance, and Health and Safety. Each of these categories has several additional measures.

Some of the key benchmarks are:

- Benchmark the performance of a specific project or company
- Benchmark evidence of value for money in procurement
- Benchmark measures other than price to support procurement decisions
- Benchmark marketing tool
- Benchmark against ISO 9001 quality management systems

Many of these measures are captured in UK National Statistics

http://www.statistics.gov.uk/hub/business-energy/production-industries/building-and-construction

Here's the real question you want to answer with benchmarking. How much does your competitor spend for tools, labor, marketing, rework etc?

Tradesman-Academy can help you determine construction business valuation...What's your business worth? What should it be worth as an optimized practice? Where to cut costs? What are my benchmarks with tips for financial performance data including revenues, expenses, and net profit/loss based on the industry such as these:

Construction Income Expense Statements		
Sales	Salary and Wages	Taxes
Depreciation	Gross Profit	Marketing
Owner compensations	Cost of Sales	Net Profit
Rent	Interest Earned	Warranty Repairs
Bad debts	Interest Expenses	

Industry Balance Sheet Benchmarks		
Cash	Inventory	Fixed Assets
Loans/Notes Payable	Receivables	Total Current Liabilities
Accounts Payable	Total Current Assets	Net Worth

Industry Financial Ratios		
Return on Sales	Quick Ratio	Current Ratio
Return on Assets	Return on Net Worth	Inventory Turnover
Assets	Sales	Net Worth

You should have a feel for performance measurement, benchmarking, and strategy growth now. A key to remember now is that a part of your strategy needs to include making your job more enjoyable. What do you do to add fun into the environment? What else needs to be included in your 90 minute chunks?

There is a reason you chose this book...you are a visionary in your trade, you wanted to learn something new, you wanted to advance your business, you have an intuitive leadership style in everything you do.

How much time did you put towards your dream today? What's the one fun thing you did today for your customers, colleagues, or an employee? Something enjoyable, but that also helped you build your business. Here's an example:

Use a local radio station advertisement focused to construction trades to register online for the weekly drawing at ...www.your company.com for doughnuts and (tea) coffee delivered to their jobsite for the work operatives. It's a great marketing technique that drives a ton of work towards your company. You get the marketing and build client relations. Upon delivery you have the opportunity to talk to potential "opportunities" for future work for your company. At a minimum they have your card in hand and will remember the "doughnuts for crews" Who do you think they'll call on the next job? It costs you in doughnuts and a one off radio advertisement, but if it results in even one job it's paid for itself.

Your strategy needs to be two-fold business and pleasure. Without one you cannot have the other. Your strategy needs to include this. People want to work with charismatic professionals.

Finally, if you use even one tip from this book then it has paid for itself and been worth your time. You owe it to yourself to visit Tradesman Academy.com

Summary of chapter 12

Your focus should center on what it takes your trade business to consistently deliver projects that provide you the profit you want to make. You need to create the most reliable process possible to deliver consistent quality with optimal profits. This involves defining your processes and delivering projects without waste. Use your 90-minute chunks per day to improve operational performance but also to build your strategy. Your key drivers are internet marketing, more services, better services, a better portfolio, better customer service, decreased cost, more efficiency, environmental and sustainability, community involvement and lean initiatives.

Remember to use key performance indicators and performance measures to tell how your company is doing. There are three types of benchmarking you can do: strategic benchmarking, process benchmarking, and performance benchmarking.

The construction and trade measures for the UK are framed under the groupings of Time, Cost, Quality, Client Satisfaction, Client

Changes, Business Performance, and Health and Safety. You have to decide how you know you are doing a good job other than we meet monthly payroll and bills.

CHAPTER 13

TOP TIPS THAT WILL SAVE YOU TIME, MONEY AND GROW YOUR BUSINESS THE OTHER GUYS DON'T KNOW OR WON'T SHARE.

Here are some great tips for your tradesman and construction business to improve cost savings, efficiency and performance that the other guys may not be using.

1. Outsource what you can – i.e. bookkeeping. Take a look at the tasks that you do throughout the day and be honest with yourself, which ones can be given to somebody else. I understand it is your business, your baby and nobody does it as conscientious as you, but you will not grow your business unless you learn to give tasks to others. As an average, a person in a well-run business is able to delegate around 80% of their work to others. If you need to pay somebody $10 per hour to do some admin work then do so, this will enable you to earn $40 per hour.

2. Keep all job costs separate and not on one job umber. I see this a lot. Let's say you do 10 jobs over a period of a month. A lot of

people calculate all the labour and materials they have purchased and carried out for the jobs as one lump sum. Doing this does not give you a true reflection on each job cost. Each job you do, open a separate job number for all allocated labour and materials to the respective job. Over a period of time you will know where you are making money and if you are losing money anywhere and more importantly which jobs are your most profitable.

3. Call tracking numbers; as mentioned in my seven secrets, you need every piece of your marketing to have a dedicated phone number to it. If you have 4 marketing pillars such as PPC, Flyers, Direct Mail and Yellow Pages advertisement, you need to find out which is working the best and concentrate on these. Call tracking numbers allow you to do this and they are very cheap, from around $3.00 per month.

4. People - People buy on how they perceive you and the level of service you offer, most will not buy on price and if they do, you don't want their work anyway as they will always find something wrong with what you have done to knock some money off so keep away from them. Present yourself to them as polite, don't talk over them, listen to their needs and concerns and demonstrate you have understood them.

5. Image - when you turn up to a job to price it, make sure your vehicle is clean and clearly signed with your company name, number and any trade industry certification all clearly visible.

Carry an ID card with you so they can easily identify you. When you enter their premises, remove your boots or put on a pair of overshoes. This will show them you have respect for their property.

6. Clear and concise quotations; Give the customer a fully documented quotation, you can have a template ready so that you can just copy and paste, however make sure you are clear with all your terms and conditions including payment as a verbal agreement doesn't carry as much weight as a written document. Make sure the price is shown clearly and they are fully aware of the cost, do not try to hide anything, if they feel you are not trust worthy, you will lose the job.

7. When quoting ask the customer how many quotes they have had or are looking at having, if they go for more than three I would be cautious as they will probably go for the cheapest, I am cheeky and I will ask what prices they have had so far, a lot will tell you when put on the spot. If they don't or say they haven't, ask them what their budget is and after they have given you a figure, follow up with the following words "Up To". Try this, and you will be surprised how many will give you information that will put you in a better position to win the job.

8. Follow up – Keep a list of jobs you price on a spreadsheet and leave around 3 days after sending the quote, give them a follow up call. You will be surprised how many people actually get work quoted for and then never have it completed.

9. Don't be a busy fool; If you get asked by a business to quote a project then set yourself a maximum amount of quotes before you start to turn work away. I have a limit of 4 quotes for any new companies that I quote for and if they do not give me any feedback or give me any work then I will move onto another company. There are a lot of businesses out there, which will use you as a pricing tool, be careful, because you will be a busy fool!

10. Work on your business and not in it. This has definitely been the biggest business growth strategy for me. Make time in your day to work on your business rather than on the shop floor. I have wrote a whole chapter on this in this book which explains what you should do with your 90 minutes, but the biggest challenge by far is you having the ability to make the time to do it, if you don't you will never have the business you desire, so please make sure you make the time.

11. Speak to your suppliers about discounts and payment terms, you need to be arranging to pay them 60 days from invoice where possible and if you give them a lot of work, as for a rebate scheme where you get a percentage of your spend back at the end of the financial year. It can add up.

12. Check with local material resource recycling centers for hard to find and unique construction project applications like doors, sinks, cabinets, windows, and tile.

13. Take advantage of the wealth of new construction estimation software for your smart phone and PC's many of which can store the information for you to work with back at the office and truly save you material calculation time.

14. Buy or Sell excess building materials online such as ebay. What are you going to do with mismatched tile and left over flooring anyway?

15. Think seasonally for purchases of tools and equipment. When will you get the best deal? You save the most money when you don't "have to" have a piece of equipment and it is on sale.

16. Can your business supply additional services to compliment your existing services; for example, If you are an electrician and you are fitting new ceiling lights to a suspended ceiling, could you change the ceiling tiles also to give a better overall look on the job.

17. Recycle material waste; such as plastics, metals, and wood a salvage or scrap yards, you can get good money for the right items.

18. Document your efforts towards recycling and reuse. These may translate into higher profits and possible tax write-offs.

19. Start each day with a detailed to-do list you want to accomplish.

20. Prioritize your day by Importance and Urgency.

21. Batch your daily tasks to speed efficiency.

22. Limit Meetings especially if you are not requesting them. They can turn into time wasters if they go on too long or happen too frequently.

23. Hire a virtual assistant to do the tasks like email, bookkeeping, customer follow-up, scheduling and research.

24. Develop templates to standardize work and improve efficiency and quality. If you have to write it over and over or on a routine basis, develop a template and print it.

25. Stay organized, nothing reduces your efficiency more including your office, shop, and storage vehicles.

26. Develop better ways to collaborate with your sub-contractors and employees for jobs including paperwork and digital communication. There is several collaboration software suppliers which help contractors and project teams to work together more efficiently by providing one stop storage for all project documentation such as Dropbox

27. Don't overschedule. It impedes on your thought process for completing work. If you keep looking at your watch because you are behind it impedes on your progress toward the task at hand.

28. Write out a zero "punch / snagging list" process and test it on your next job. What will it take to get to this point?

29. In one of your 90 minute chunks make a complete review of the entire list of jobs you have done over the last quarter. Correct any estimation variances that were over 3%.

30. Always identify your equipment and tools. Keep the serial numbers on file back at your office and engrave high value items if they have no numeric identifier. It helps to have pictures of your equipment too including trailers, pipe threaders, conduit benders, loaders etc. Make sure you insure your tools as well. A small amount of insurance affords you good piece of mind in the event they go missing.

31. Always explain your work to the customer in domestic jobs. This maintains their confidence and helps ease any concerns. They may not understand phases of work or how new work and remodel work tie together. Many domestic customers will tell you directly they cannot understand or visualize what you are trying to do from prints or drawings. They may need some explanation of how things tie together or what the next steps are.

32. Always ask for feedback on the finished job regardless of compliments or complaints. Both of these will help you develop and improve your business.

33. Arrange your invoicing process so that invoices are sent on the same day weekly and make sure that it is done religiously to your customer upon completion of your work.

34. Take advantage of free software on the Internet that can help you build your business. Use trial software to find out what works for you and to see if it has a good fit for your business before you make an actual purchase.

35. Try swapping work or bartering with like trades. If you are an electrical trade company and need a small plumbing job on your project see if you can trade work and negotiate a savings.

36. Join tradesmen organizations for your trade. They may have a membership fee but often offer substantial savings for trade related purchases or insurance pricing.

37. Periodically use your 90 minute chunks to review your overhead costs including insurance, office rental, cellular phones, gas and diesel costs as well as ongoing contracts you may have. See what other alternatives are available.

CHAPTER 14

BUSINESS PLAN DEVELOPMENT

This chapter is for those who are new to the trades and construction company business and require a business plan to acquire startup funding. You should have some written plan whether starting or expanding your business. Not everyone needs a business plan but this is a natural bridge to funding if you do need it. Access to funding is a key concern of construction and trade businessmen according to UK business surveys. Banks and lenders will require a business plan outlining your business structure and operations. This plan shows the lender your level of seriousness and preparedness to manage a business. The plan will typically contain the sections, which show a summary of your business, your goals and mission, a market analysis, and budget/cash flow analysis. The basic sections and requirements are outlined for you.

Business information includes

   Company name

   Address

   Telephone number

   Owner Contact Information

Executive Summary

The executive summary succinctly outlines your business goals for your company and necessary financing to operate the business as outlined. Business experts recommend you write this section last not first so you have a complete understanding of the business requirements. Basically this is your sales pitch to lenders.

The Description of the Business

This section describes the type of business, the services it provides, and what your business offers compared to competitors. This section will describe your experience and expertise.

Strategic Plan and Direction

This section outlines your vision and how you plan to achieve your goal. This will include your plan for business growth, profit estimations, and employees.

This section of the plan will explain the experience of the business owners. (Explaining why you should be in this business)

Financial documents with proforma information and financial projections. These outline your financial plans and goals for income, revenue, and, return on investments.

You then provide analysis of risks and opportunities, strengths, and weaknesses for your company. Explain how you will mitigate risks.

Business Structure Description

In the business structure, formally describe the initial structure for the business, experience, and completed projects. This is a synopsis of your company describing how long you have been in business and some company background. You will describe the structure of your business such as partnership, limited liability etc.

Describe you company's mission and vision statement. What is your business philosophy and where do you plan to take your business?

In this section you will also describe your services, market, profit analysis, and what you bring to the community.

Markets and Competition

Explain your marketing for the business using the tips you have learned. This includes the opportunities you will engage. Locations you will work, current economic trends, your growth potential, any niche markets, and your bidding process. Include any seasonal or market fluctuations.

You are required to show projected revenues in one year and five year scenarios showing best and worst case scenarios

Marketing plan

In the marketing plan you will include your market research, surveys, opportunity in targeted areas. What are you doing for Search Engine Optimization? What markets do you target:

building owners, government, real estate developers, brokers, or architects?

What is your pricing strategy? What are your costs, desired profits, and who are your competition, image portrayal.

Your marketing strategy should include all of the information we have discussed to include mailing, internet, direct marketing, brochures, business cards, and email.

Organizational structure and business operations

In this section you will include an organizational chart of your operations and any employees.

How you approach risk management and professional liability. What claims have you made and what is your safety record?

Explain your planning strategy and how you bid jobs. How do you do project selection and bidding and buyout processes are organized and managed.

Company benefits

What advantages do you have? Location, specialized construction equipment, specialized experience or project management.

Financial components

Provide a history of your businesses financial statements which include balance sheets, expenses, revenues, and profits.

Appendices of the plan

The appendices are the location to house relevant information to support your plan such as financial spreadsheets, references, insurance and bond certificates, resumes and any additional supporting information.

What Tradesman Academy Can do for you?

The Tradesman Academy can help you develop your trade business better than any other resource out there. The tools, tips, and resources that are available on the site are based on tried and true methods for growing the best possible business you can whether you want to start a new business, grow an existing one, build a better financial future, or build a better lifestyle balance.

The Tradesman Academy shows you the best ways to improve your efficiency, productivity, quality, and profit including complex operations such as marketing; with detailed instructions on how to build your website and search engine optimization (SEO). Let us show you the tips you need and traps that caused the failure of your competition.

We can show you where to start. How to structure your business. How to market, price, and source jobs. We also show you how to strategically position your business to be the best in your location. Our strategic methods help you with financial control, project delivery, quality indicators, green initiatives, process improvement, scheduling, and cost reductions.

It all boils down to how you are using your 90 minute chunks to grow your business and having the right tools in one place to do it from. We encourage you to grow your business at Tradesman Academy and look forward to working with you to start and build your business.

Let's get started

About the Author:

David Lee is the founder and owner of Tradesman Academy and author of the book "From Tradesman to a Businessman" "How tradesman make their first million in 90 minute chunks"

Founded in 2014 to help tradesman and tradeswomen build a business in modern society that is successful for their needs, whether that be personal gratification, wealth or lifestyle. David has worked in and run businesses that have encompassed a variety of wants from the people he has worked with, and met that have in their own trade businesses become successful.

David has been working within the trade industry for over 20 years from leaving school at 16, David trained as an electrician and qualified at the age of 20 following which he decided to expand his knowledge with further education and gaining qualifications as an engineer and additional subjects including health & safety and marketing. He has worked within 5 large companies educating himself on the things that do work and those that don't. David has since built two separate million plus businesses both within four years of starting them. He now plans to focus on helping other quality tradesmen and women build their own successful businesses and lead the life they desire.

If you would like more information on the topics discussed in this book, please visit www.tradesman-academy.com

Whatever you decide, I wish you success, fulfillment and achievement of your desires.

27930140R00097

Made in the USA
Middletown, DE
26 December 2015